M000199592

Claim Your Connection

A practical guide to giving

the best presentation of your life,

unaffected by fear,

in any circumstances

Gary Stine

Spoken Word Solutions
63 North River Road
Fort Edward, NY 12828

Copyright 2014 Gary Stine
All rights reserved
Jacket design: Lorena Vogeler
Typography: Brian P. Lawler
Cover photo: Angela Caputo
Published 2014
ISBN 978-0-985-1019-4-7

A Few Words About the Title
and Purpose of this Book

Contrary to popular belief, the connection between speaker and audience doesn't need to be created, because it already exists. It only needs to be claimed, and it's up to the speaker to do this. This is also the source of power for a speaker. This book is designed to put that power squarely in your hands.

My job is to enable you to give presentations at a level beyond which you thought you were capable, whatever your starting point may be. Another vital component of my job is to enable you to give presentations uncompromised by any sort of fear. You may still experience fear in certain presentational circumstances, but it doesn't need to dilute the experience of you or your audience, or to diminish your effectiveness as a presenter.

Because I respect your time, I have no desire to waste it. This book is a distillation of what I've learned and taught through many years. As a distillation, all that's non-essential has been removed. What's left is what you need to know, and what is seldom, if ever, addressed. The chapters are designed to be as short as possible. My goal is to give you help you may not have known was available, and I offer it to you sincerely, and with respect.

CHAPTER 1:

Fear of Presenting is Only Misplaced Focus

You'll probably find the focus of this book different from what you've heard in the past. Most presentational learning talks primarily about information and about ways of delivering it. That's fine, and we'll be dealing with that, but we're going to be talking about what's going on underneath the surface, both for the presenter, and for the audience. Presentational learning doesn't usually deal with the deeper issues, and that creates situations that can backfire, or spin out of control. The overall goal here is to make it possible for you to fearlessly present the *real you*, in front of any audience, in any circumstances, to save you hours of preparation time, and to help you define what you really want out of a presentation, so that you're more likely to get whatever that is.

Along the way, we'll talk about what's really going on, and what's really at stake when you stand in front of an audience and present, and I'll help you to have the same level of comfort and accessibility in front of an audience that you do with close friends. In other words, we'll focus on *how to be yourself* in front of an audience, any audience, in any circumstances. We'll also work on helping you to be able to present in a clear, concise, compelling fashion that builds trust between you and your audience.

Whenever you give a talk or a presentation, there are certain elements you can control, and certain elements you can't. In my experience, people tend to put too much focus on the uncontrollable elements and too little on the controllable elements, which are your goals, your intention, and your connection to the audience. Focus on these elements will take most of the fear out of any presentation, and will enable you to be at your most effective in any combination of difficult circumstances. Just to be clear, we won't be concentrating on how to give a PowerPoint presentation. That information is widely available; what I'm about to talk to you about is not. As a tool, PowerPoint is fine, but it is almost always used by presenters to hide from their audience in some way. (You may know the feeling; "As long as I have my slides, I'll be OK.") Most or all of what you've heard in the past probably doesn't deal with the true source of power and influence in a presentation, which is letting the real you be seen, and allowing that real you to establish a strong connection to your audience. Nor does it deal directly with the main issue for most presenters, which is some manifestation of fear, and some degree of fear.

Let's talk about both the real you and fear of presenting, because they're closely connected to one another. Your power as a presenter is based largely on your ability to make a human connection with the audience. When an audience sees you give a presentation, whether they know it or not, they're hoping to see the real you, the one with nothing to fear and nothing to hide. What they don't want to see is a fear-driven, superficial version of you doing an imitation of the real you, and if that's what you're doing, the audience will know it instinctively. Presenters hide in plain sight from their audiences in the hope of feeling safe, because they mistakenly believe they'll be harshly judged if they show who they really are. In fact, you'll be judged much more harshly if you attempt to hide who you are, and because you will have failed to make a strong connection with the audience, you won't achieve you goals, and they're likely to walk away with nothing. So, here's the choice you have in the simplest terms: You can risk nothing and hang on to the illusion of safety, effectively deadening yourself to your audience, or you can take a risk, show them how alive you are, and have the opportunity to really enter and influence the consciousness of each audience member. You get to choose, but understand, it will be one or the other.

For a presenter, the first few seconds in front of an audience usually are the most intimidating. These first few seconds are also the most important. If you're able to show them the real you, in other words, simply let them into the flow of life that's already going through you, you'll be well on your way to making a strong connection. It's common for presenters, even highly experienced ones, to try a little too hard in these crucial first moments, and so they *manufacture* their flow of life instead of just letting it out. Think of it like turning on a movie or video. The movie or video you're about to watch is already there when you turn it on. Turning on the TV just gives you access to it. The flow of life going through you is already there. You're just giving that flow to the audience.

If what I'm asking of you sounds like a lot to expect, don't worry, we'll get you there. Believe it or not, you already have what you need in order to show them the real you. We're going to focus on tools designed to release that real you. The more willing you are to claim your connection with the audience, to show them the real you, the easier you make it for them to see you as someone who is *like them*, and someone who is in fact, *one of them*. It's ironic, isn't it? Showing them what's different about you actually links you to them. Another way to say this is, showing them what's unique about you allows them to see what's universal about you. So your willingness to show them the real you allows them to identify with you. This happens because they'll very quickly start to feel like they know you, which makes it possible for them to trust you. As I've already said, until they trust you, they won't be completely open to what you have to tell them. We'll be focusing on making this human connection. It's easier to make than you might think. As a matter of complete truth, the connection between you and your audience is already there. You're not establishing something new as much as you're revealing something that already exists. Without this connection, you're just mouthing information, and your presentation will never really get off the ground.

If connecting on the level I've just talked about is so important, why don't more presenters let their audiences see who they really are? You already know the answer, and it's simple. Fear is what keeps most presentations from being compelling. Fear is what keeps most presenters from revealing who they really are in a way that connects them to their audience, and allows an open channel of communication. Fear of presenting exists in any number of forms and degrees. Don't worry, fear can be dealt with very successfully. I've watched and coached so many hundreds of clients giving thousands of presentations that I've gotten to be very good at seeing just how much fear is coming through in a presentation, even when people are good at hiding it. We're not going to be talking about hiding it, because that doesn't really work, and it certainly doesn't work in really stressful or high-stakes situations. Besides, being filled with fear feels awful anytime, especially when you're trying to give a presentation, and it certainly doesn't allow you to be at your best and to show the real you.

For our purposes, I want you to think of fear of presenting, whatever the source of that fear may be, simply as misplaced focus. I'm not minimizing fear; I'm talking about how to reclaim your power as a presenter by minimizing the effect fear has on you. Since presenting the real you at your very best is our common goal, we're going to address presentational fear at its source. Your fear might seem very individual to you, and some of the specifics attached to it certainly are, but the essential nature of the fear you may feel about presenting, even if you only experience it under particular conditions, has more in common with what we all experience than you may know. We'll be talking about the source of this fear shortly.

By the way, please don't worry if you feel that presentations aren't your greatest strength, and if you have trouble imagining that you can ever be a really good, interesting, compelling presenter. The best presenters I know aren't the ones to whom it came naturally; the best are the ones who had to overcome some difficulty, or some fear, and understand exactly how they're able to do what they're doing when they present. It certainly didn't come naturally to me. I struggled to be able to stand in front of an audience, and to be able to bring them along with me on my journey, and into my reality. Knowing how to do something is fine, but understanding exactly how you're able to do it, regardless of the circumstances you may find yourself in, is much more valuable because it allows you to replicate the experience. It took me many years to learn this, and my intention is to save you a great deal of time, and to help you leave behind any fear you might have about presenting. I'm grateful to have been able to do this in a one-on-one situation with hundreds of clients, and I'm happy to help you get there.

So let's start at the beginning. Presentations, in whatever form they appear, one-to-group, or one-on-one are not primarily about information, as you may have been led to believe. Presentations are always about connecting to an audience, about revealing yourself as a human being and allowing them to trust you. The flow of information is just a by-product of this human connection. You may be speaking in an intelligent, coherent way, your slides may be great, but until you establish trust, the audience isn't open to or absorbing anything you say. It's your job to allow them to recognize your humanity, and to make them feel comfortable about trusting you. It doesn't happen by accident. By the way, I want to be very clear that when I use the expression, *recognizing your humanity*, I'm not talking about some kind of presentation that's removed from the everyday world of high-level business presentations. Even in that particular world, where I've done most of my presentation work, maybe especially in the business world, in order for an audience to be open to your message and your information, they *have* to be able to recognize you as someone who is courageous enough to confront them and connect to them. Simply put, you won't get to them on an intellectual level until you get to them on an emotional level. The sort of recognition I'm referring to occurs very quickly, within seconds, and we'll talk about how it happens and what you can do to make sure that it happens.

CHAPTER 2:

Your First Obligation

Your first obligation as a presenter is to claim your connection with the audience. Out of that connection comes trust. No connection, no trust. No trust in you by the audience leads to no connection to whatever it is that you're presenting, which leads to no acceptance or absorption of your presentation. The result is that your audience (of any size, even an audience of one) is the same at the end of your presentation as they were at the beginning. The only reason you're ever in front of an audience is to change them in some way. It might be subtle, it might be dramatic, but you always want to change either their perception or their behavior. You want them to have a slightly different world view when they leave the room.

There's no reason for an audience to trust a presenter who doesn't make his or her humanity visible and accessible, and until you do this, the audience can't trust you, because you haven't given them an opportunity. When I say, *make your humanity visible,* all I mean is to have the courage to allow yourself to be recognized by the audience, and the courage to let them into your reality. This is a crucial point, so to make it completely clear, think of meeting someone or seeing them give a presentation, and feeling like you already know them. This feeling has happened to all of us, and happens often. What's important to understand is that it doesn't happen by sheer chance. It happens because the person standing in front of you isn't protecting herself from you in a way that cuts you off from her.

The feeling that we need to protect ourselves when we stand up in front of others and speak is as common as it is untrue. You have nothing to protect for the simple reason that the audience can't take anything real away from you, even though it may seem that way. This is one of the primary, universal sources of fear when it comes to speaking in public: *They'll take something away from me. They'll diminish me somehow.* There's nothing an audience can do that will make you any less than you are at that moment (even if they were to laugh at you, which I'll talk about later). Once you realize the absolute truth of that, you don't have anything to protect, and they're able to recognize you as someone they have something in common with. At that point, and only at that point, trust can be established, and real communication can start.

Trust can be generated in the first few seconds of a presentation. As a matter of fact, it has to be generated then, because if it isn't done right at the beginning, you've lost them. Attention spans are getting shorter all the time, (this becomes more true the higher you go on an organizational ladder) so you have a really short time to accomplish a number of things. As I said, the first thing an audience is looking for (though they don't know this on a conscious level) is whether or not you are willing to look them in the eye and make a human connection. Like a number of principles I'll be talking about, this is less about what you do physically than it is about the intention that you have in mind. If you understand on a fundamental level that you have nothing to protect, and you have a clear, strong intention to make a connection, and you trust that intention, the rest will pretty much take care of itself. Trusting the intention is the key. So it's much less about mechanics than it is about intention. That can be hard for people to accept. Very often they want the ABCs of how to make the connection, and that's easy to understand. What can be easily quantified has a great deal of appeal, especially in situations that generate fear. What's harder to quantify, like an intention, feels less safe. It's simply not true. Believe me, if your intention is to connect, that's the first and most important thing. When you have that clear intention, what comes across to the audience is something like, *I have nothing to hide. Come on in to my reality.* At that point you're essentially holding up a mirror to the audience that allows them to see their humanity in you. Then they can look at you and know that you're willing to reveal yourself to them.

When you've set up that situation, trust can follow very quickly. You see this either happening or not happening in politics all the time. Here's an example that's still fairly fresh in people's minds: in the presidential election of 2012, Mitt Romney was never able to reveal his humanity; he wasn't able *to let us come inside*. Instead, he held us at arm's length. People sensed this on an unconscious level, though they might not have been able to put it into words. Barack Obama is very comfortable revealing his humanity; it was one of the reasons he was elected. He was willing to *let us come in*. He showed himself to us, and it made us feel like we knew him, and so we were willing to trust him.

Just to repeat, information only flows when an audience is receptive and accessible. The common view is that these qualities are a matter of chance; that sometimes the audience is accessible, and sometimes they aren't. This isn't true. As the presenter, you're responsible for the receptiveness and accessibility of the audience. You create this atmosphere by showing them that you're completely receptive and accessible to them. Audiences are very smart on an unconscious level, and are waiting for you to model the behavior you want from them. They don't know this on a conscious level, and they don't need to. Next time you see a really good presenter, pay attention to the first few minutes, and you may be aware of the sensation of willingly giving yourself over to him or her. In other words, the presenter made him or herself completely accessible and receptive to the audience, completely connected to them. This can't be faked, and there's no reason to try. Trying to fake a connection never works, and is embarrassing to watch. If you're watching for this connection closely, as it happens, you may be aware of a sense of relief on the part of the audience that the presenter has modeled this behavior, this receptiveness and accessibility, and that now you as an audience member know what the presenter expects from you. Individual audience members and the audience as a whole are just waiting for this kind of signal. That's when the connection that already exists between presenter and audience is revealed and claimed, and when trust is born.

Incidentally, when you, as the presenter feel this connection starting to happen, when you know that the audience is with you, and willing to be taken where you lead them, you'll be aware that whatever fear you might have is evaporating. Your willingness to claim this connection with the audience blurs the lines between you and them. Instead of *me* and *them*, it starts to feel more like *us*, which is how it has to be. After all, you and the audience are on a journey together. You want to be able to feel like *us*. This is a wonderful feeling, and carries with it the obligation to be respectful and completely honest with your audience. Incidentally, it's the moment when you start to feel like *us* rather than *me* and *them* that self-consciousness starts to disappear.

As I've said, until you trust a presenter, you're not going to be fully receiving what she has to give you. You'll be hearing bits and pieces, but you're not really going to be fully connected, and so you'll be missing a huge part of what's being conveyed. It's always about reaching both their hearts and minds. Reaching just their minds (or just their hearts) won't keep them connected to you for the length of your presentation. It's crucial to understand this. It's always true, even in the driest scientific presentation you can imagine.

Your first obligation is to claim this connection I've just described. There's nothing magical or mystical about claiming it. This, as far as I'm concerned, is one of the primary rules, maybe *the* primary rule of human relationships: Give what you want to get in return. If you want receptiveness and accessibility, give them first. If you want trust, or respect, give them first. You can't expect to get from a relationship what you haven't given. Your relationship with an audience is no different than any other human relationship. All right, it's a little different in that you're having what I like to call a simultaneous series of one-on-one relationships with a number of people, maybe even a large number of people, but it's still essentially a relationship, even though it might only last for the length of your presentation. Give what you want to get back from them, and give it the second you step before your audience. If you're focused on them, on what you have for them, and on what you want to give them, in other words, focused on the atmosphere you intend to create, and focused on your goals (which we'll talk about at some length) you won't have the burden of thinking or worrying about yourself. I'll talk more about this later on, but the point I've just made about focus is actually the way to make any amount of presentational fear evaporate. Learning to focus your complete attention on the audience, their needs, and the goals that you've set up for yourself will keep you on a firm, calm footing, and won't give you any time to be thinking about yourself or about any fear you may have.

CHAPTER 3:

The Root of All Presentational Fear

The root of all fear when you stand before an audience has a single source, but has multiple variations. I'm sure that this will sound familiar once I say it, because it probably will have happened to you in the past, or once in a while, or on a regular basis. It begins with the feeling that you may not be good enough, or interesting enough, or know enough; at any rate, some version of *not being enough.* This leads you on a downward spiral. The next thing that happens within you is that you see the situation in terms of *me* and *them.* This is a totally arbitrary division, and a creation of your fear. It's not real, but it seems like the most real thing in the world at that moment. As I said earlier, you and the audience are actually always *we* or *us.* The relationship between you is never actually *me and them,* or worse still *me versus them.*

The point where you create the artificial division between *me* and *them* is when extreme self-consciousness takes hold, and you may find yourself thinking thoughts like, *That was the wrong word; I shouldn't have said that, I wonder if they can see me sweating, why isn't she paying attention, why is this person typing a text message* and on and on and on. When this happens, it begins to feel to you like it's not really even you standing there anymore. It's someone less than you; some half-awake impostor pretending to be you. That's the way it can seem to the audience, too. It simply doesn't have to be this way. We've already started to talk about how to leave this paralyzing fear behind, and we'll be talking more about it. For now, be open to incorporating this concept into your reality: don't confuse your self with your self-consciousness. Self-consciousness is not who you are, it's only a feeling you may be having. With the proper tools and perspective, the amount of power you allow it to have over you is completely within your control.

From my point of view, there's simply no such thing as an informational presentation. I said earlier that you as the presenter are always trying to change the audience in some way; to change their thinking, to change their point of view, to change their perception, to give guidance that will change their behavior or inform a decision. At the very least, you're trying to infect them with the same level of passion that you feel about a particular subject. Information is just one part of the vehicle that accomplishes this. But, be really clear: regardless of what you've heard all your life, a presentation is not really about information.

CHAPTER 4:

Passion

Whoever you are, you're a compelling human being. You may not think of yourself that way, but you are. There's only one thing that can keep you or keep others from seeing you as a compelling, interesting human being, and that's when you hold back your passion, or are disconnected from it. This is a very common expression of fear that could be stated as, *if I show them my passion, I'm afraid they might laugh at me.* That possibility exists, though it's much more remote than you might think. Even if they *did* laugh at you, at least they'd be engaged, at least you'd have their full attention, and you'd have an opportunity to make a strong connection and impression. By the way, if an audience ever laughs at you, join them in laughing. You'll show that you have a sense of humor about yourself, which is very endearing to an audience. When you do that, you show them not only your humanity, but that you're one of them, and they'll be instantly *in your corner.* Starting to laugh with an audience you may feel is laughing at you instantly transforms the situation from *me and them* to *us.*

The only difference between presenters who appear to be interesting, and those who don't, is that the *interesting* ones are connected to their passion, and are willing to share it with the audience. In fact, they can't wait to share it with the audience. By being willing to share their passion, they show us who they are as people; they reveal themselves to us, and make it possible for us to trust them. The *uninteresting* ones are either disconnected from their passion or are unable to share it with an audience. By failing to reveal their passion to the audience, they fail to reveal themselves. The result is that they don't allow us to connect to their humanity.

What disconnects you from passion is self-consciousness, which is a form of fear. Self-consciousness destroys passion, or at least temporarily displaces it. Would you rather listen to someone who had no emotional connection to what they were talking about, or to someone who was passionately connected to what they were talking about, and was determined to have you, as an audience member, feel that same level of passion? This is particularly true in presentations of a technical nature. The more technical the nature of your presentation, the more important that you be willing to show your passion about your subject, so that the audience has a chance to connect to your message on an emotional level. Just to be clear, when I say *be willing to show your passion*, I don't mean jumping up and down and running back and forth. I mean being willing to feel your passion and being willing to allow your passion to be visible as you stand in front of your audience. If you allow yourself to deeply connect to your passion, it will be seen and felt by the audience without any artificial jumping up and down, which is just an imitation of passion. Like all imitations, imitation passion looks ridiculous next to the real thing.

CHAPTER 5:

Conversational and Presentational Personae

I often tell clients that after talking to them for less than five minutes, I know more about the way they come across to the world than they'll ever know, because I'm looking from a much more objective vantage point than they are. In other words, I'm looking from outside of them, and based on my experience, I happen to know what I'm looking at. What I start to see in those first five minutes (or less) is what I call their *conversational persona*. This is the everyday *you* that you present to the world; the comfortable, relaxed, informal *you*. This is generally the version of you that doesn't feel the need to hide, or to protect itself. This persona is probably very close to the way you see yourself, and would like to be seen by others. Some of us, not very many, are pretty much the same no matter who we're with, and no matter what the circumstances. These are people who only have what could be called a conversational persona, and they're comfortable showing it in any situation.

Most of us have other personae, and most of us have what I call a *presentational persona*. This persona tends to be a little more formal, more reserved, more is held back. When this persona takes over, what you might consider to be the real you isn't as immediately apparent. In most of us, there is a difference, sometimes a big difference, between the conversational persona, the nice, easy, relaxed, open you, and the presentational persona, the more held back, tucked-in you, the more guarded you. If you were going to some social event that was important to you, and you had control of which of these two personae you were going to bring along (and it could only be one) which one would you take?

You'd probably take the conversational persona, because it's so much more accessible, and would probably be more likely to make a good impression, to make a connection with people, to make friends, and to make you more comfortable than the presentational persona would. What I'm suggesting to you is that you *do have control* over which of these you choose when you have to present to an audience, or have a job interview, or a meeting. What I'm really suggesting is that the two, the conversational, and the presentational, have to be so congruent that they become one, or just slightly different versions of the same one. The point is, your humanity has to be as apparent in your presentational persona as it is in your everyday, totally accessible, conversational persona. Your willingness to show the parts of yourself that you value most highly is the key to being sure your conversational persona is the one who shows up. One of the things we'll be working toward is making the distance between these two personae fade away.

It might be useful to start by talking about what makes the two personae different. If the conversational persona is the most comfortable version of you, the presentational persona is the one that's been affected, to some degree, by fear of one kind or another. These are the fear-forms that I mentioned earlier, and I'm sure that some of them will sound familiar: Fear of not being good enough, fear of not receiving acceptance or approval, fear that you'll sound like you don't know what you're talking about, that you won't sound intelligent, fear that you might not get what you want, fear that you *might* get what you want, fear that you won't live up to your own expectations or the expectations of others, fear of not being attractive enough, and on and on and on. The common theme is fear of *not being enough.* Sound familiar? This is what we do to ourselves when we have to appear in front of others. Every self-doubt we've ever had can come up, we focus on these doubts, and what happens is that the doubts, or fears, essentially cripple us, and make us seem like something or someone other than, or something less than what we actually are. Have you ever had the experience of watching a presenter, someone you knew, maybe even knew well, and saw that person crippled by fear and self-doubt to the point where it seemed like a different person than the one you knew? Have you ever been presenting and become gripped by fear to the point where it no longer felt like it was you giving the presentation?

I think we've all had that experience at one time or another. The really good part is that you don't ever have to do that to yourself again (and just to be clear, it is something that you're doing to yourself, even though you're probably not aware of it).

I want to talk about shyness for just a minute. Shyness is an exaggerated form of the self-consciousness that most of us have or have had in some situation or another. A lot of people are shy. I was for a big part of my life. Someone told me years ago that shyness is its own punishment, and now I know that's true. Shyness is also an expression of fear. I was forced to deal with my shyness because at the time, I happened to be a professional actor and that crippling shyness kept me from being able to display my ability as an actor. If you were to meet me now, it would be hard for you to ever believe that I had been paralyzed by shyness. The only reason that I mention it is, because I had to overcome crippling shyness, I know what it takes to do that, and I can help you to do the same thing, or to overcome any sort of self-consciousness or other form of fear that keeps you from being the real you in front of an audience. Shyness and self-consciousness aren't really that different from one another, and they both have the same origin, so for our purposes, I'll be referring to them interchangeably. Don't worry if you're shy, and don't worry if you're afraid; in the long run, neither of them really matter. Neither of these conditions need to be permanent, nor will they stand in the way of your being an effective presenter if you follow the guidelines we'll be discussing.

CHAPTER 6:

A Presentation is Always a Conversation

When we talk about goals a little later on, you'll get a great tool to help you to make that initial connection, and the *how to* of creating that connection will be clearer. For now, I'm going to talk about the physical aspects of how to do it. The very first thing, when you walk into a room for a meeting, or walk on a stage, or are introduced for a presentation, is to really take in the audience with not only your eyes, but with all your senses, and with your whole being. Acknowledge them, take them in, and savor your opportunity to infect them with your passion. (As I mentioned, this is true no matter how *dry* or dispassionate the material that you're presenting may be.) Confront them with your eyes. The alternative, and I'm sure everyone has seen this, and maybe even done it, is to kind of pretend that the audience isn't really there, or at least to pretend that you're not about to enter into a relationship with them and go on a journey with them. I keep saying audiences are very smart on a subconscious level, and when you start talking to them without acknowledging their presence, they'll very likely read it as disrespect or as an announcement by you that you're not really looking for a connection. You probably wouldn't do that in a regular conversation, and a presentation is always a conversation, even if you're doing all, or most of the talking. It's still an exchange, because as you talk, or give to them, you're also taking from them. You're taking in their level of comprehension, their level of interest, their level of engagement, and you're adjusting your presentation accordingly.

So, if respect is what you want, and every presenter wants that, deliver respect by openly acknowledging the fact that you're standing in front of a crowd of living, breathing human beings. This only takes a second; as a matter of fact, you can do it as you are walking to the podium, or the microphone, or the center of the room, depending on what the setup is. You can even do it if you're sitting around a table and will be presenting from where you're sitting. In this case, it takes even less time. It can literally be done in half a second, and will be one of the best investments of time you ever make.

Incidentally, the only situation in which you can conceivably get away with starting your presentation without acknowledging the audience and consciously setting up an atmosphere of mutual respect is an academic presentation or any other where you really have a captive audience, and I mean captive, in other words, where attendance is mandatory and getting up and leaving is not an option. Even in those situations, the likelihood of people connecting to you so that they can absorb your message will be enhanced by setting up an atmosphere of respect.

Looking into the eyes of an audience, looking for an indication of connection and comprehension in every set of eyes you can see is one of the most important things you can do, and one of the first things you have to do. Sometimes presenters are convinced that in order to be able to think on their feet, they have to be looking at the ceiling, or the floor, or at a blank wall. This is only a habit, and can easily be replaced by a more productive habit. Having gotten used to really looking into the eyes of an audience, I actually find it easier to think when I'm looking at them. Looking deeply into the eyes of an audience sounds scary to people who aren't used to doing it. I've even heard people suggest that a presenter focus on the exit signs in the back of the auditorium. I guess that might work, if your only goal is to get through your presentation and head for the exit. If you want to make a difference, if you want to change the audience in some way, to change their perception or behavior, looking at the exit signs is a sure way to accomplish nothing. It's a form of denial, of pretending that you're not really in front of the audience. I'm not a big fan of denial. In my experience, acknowledging a situation as it really is works much better than denial. Once you become used to looking into the eyes of an audience, it becomes incredibly reassuring and it gets you a number of things in return. It gets you information as to their comprehension and level of engagement, as I've already said, and it gets you their trust and respect, because they'll read direct contact as an indication of your trust and respect for them. It gives you something else that's the most reassuring of all. It reminds you that you're dealing with *individuals* who happen to be in the same place at the same time. One of the most destructive illusions is to view an audience as *they* or *them,* as a sort of monolithic consciousness. There is no they, there is no them; there is only a collection of individuals, with individual reactions. Continually reminding yourself of this by making eye contact with as many individual audience members as you possibly can keeps you calm and focused. It also reinforces your sense of you and the audience combining to form *we* or *us.* By the way, you can test the truth of this last statement very easily. The next time you're an audience member, be aware of your reactions to the presentation being given. Notice that your reactions are your reactions, not the reactions of a collective. At times, your reactions may intersect with those of the larger audience, but on some level, they will always be your personal reactions. That's true of every single audience member. An audience is a collection of individuals, with individual reactions. There is no *they* there is no *them,* there is no monolithic consciousness.

I've talked about how important it is for you to connect with the audience, so that they can trust you, recognize their own humanity in you, and be completely open to what you have for them. Making the connection is at least as important for you as the presenter. The self-consciousness that comes from the idea that there's *me* and there's *them* becomes, in the stressful situation that presentations represent for most people, an artificial wall between *me* and *them.* It starts to feel higher and more impenetrable than it really is, and so the self-consciousness feeds on itself and gains strength. This is the point we've already talked about, where you become so self-conscious it may seem to you that it's no longer you giving the presentation. This is also the point where you've lost control.

Here's what's happening in the situation I've just described. You've focused on what it feels like, on how nervous you are, on how difficult it is, on whether or not you're getting it *right*, and you've essentially shut out the audience. You no longer have a connection to them or a relationship with them. Your relationship at that moment is only with yourself and your fear. Here's one of the most important things I have to share with you: You're most like yourself when you're thinking least about yourself. When you're not thinking about yourself, the more spontaneous, flexible, engaged, real, and *in the moment* you're able to be. The more you think about yourself, (focusing on how you look, on whether you picked the wrong phrase, the wrong outfit, on whether or not the audience likes you, and so on) the *less* like yourself you seem.

An example that beautifully illustrates this has to do with young kids. I'm sure you've all seen this, whether it has been your own kids, or with younger brothers or sisters, or nieces and nephews. It happens whenever you have a special connection to a child. When you haven't seen them for a while (sometimes it's only for a few hours) they may have seen something happen, or have experienced something that they *can't wait* to tell you about. They have to share it with you, and nothing will stop them. Their job is to get you as excited about their news as they are. When you watch a child communicate on this level, there's a complete and total lack of self-consciousness, in the truest sense of the term. They're simply not conscious of themselves; they're focused completely on you, and are only conscious of sharing their experience or their news with you.

I can almost feel you smiling with recognition, because we've all seen this lovely phenomenon many times. The child seems like his original, authentic self because he isn't thinking about himself. He's only focused on his connection with you and on what he needs to communicate. Kids in this state seem incredibly alive and real, and it's easy to connect to the humanity the two of you share. In this situation, a *we* has been created out of two people. Unfortunately, this absence of self-consciousness tends to go away when kids hit puberty. In fact, it goes to the other extreme. Most people never really get it back. Some large degree of it can be gotten back, and it's really just a matter of being willing to give yourself over to that connection to the audience and to your need to get them enlisted in your cause (even if your cause seems to be dry and technical.) This takes a certain amount of trust on the part of a presenter, but once you do it, you never have to go back to that paralyzing sense of self-consciousness. Once you've chosen to make a connection on that level, it becomes a choice that's always available to you.

CHAPTER 7:

Your Second Obligation:
Setting Up a Compelling Reality

All I've been talking about up until now is making that connection in the first few seconds of your presentation, or meeting, or interview, or whatever situation it may be. Even though there are differences in each of these encounters, they're more alike than they are different, and in each of them, it's your responsibility to make the connection to the people who you're talking with. After you've made the sort of initial contact that lets your audience know you're committed to having an open channel of communication with them, one of the primary tools in securing that connection is in letting your audience know what you have for them. This actually leads into the second obligation you have to your audience, which is to set up a more compelling reality than they already have going on in their minds. People love to stay in their own thoughts, in their own self-designed realities, and almost all of us do this until someone or something presents us with a reality more compelling than the one already going on in our own minds. This is exactly what happens when you find yourself channel-surfing. How long do you give each channel before you move on to the next? A few seconds, at most; sometimes less. The question that you might be asking yourself when you channel surf, whether you know it or not, is this: *Is the reality being presented to me on this channel more compelling than the one that's already going on in my head?* If the answer is no, you move on to the next channel. When you're watching a presentation, the same process is going on. If the presenter doesn't bring you into a compelling reality very quickly, you stay with your own reality, in other words, you stay inside your own thoughts.

There are several other unconscious questions audience members are asking themselves: *Does this presenter have anything for me? Does this presentation have anything to do with me?* Unless the audience members can answer these questions by saying, *yes,* they stay right where they are, in their own minds. An audience will be a little more patient with a presenter than when they're channel surfing, but not much more. You don't have any longer than about 30 seconds. As a presenter, your sense of intention has to be ironclad. You have to know exactly what you're there to give them, and what you want from them, and you have to start to give it to them right away.

When you stand in front of an audience and start to talk, there are as many *realities* in the room as there are people in the audience. Each of us tends to have an internal focus that often has little to do with what's going on outside of our minds. We're thinking about all the things we have to do later, about what we're going to do when the weekend comes, about a disagreement we had with someone earlier in the day, about any number of things that are disconnected from what's happening around us. In this situation, a presenter has to bring audience members into his or her reality in a compelling way, otherwise, the audience members will appear to be paying attention, but will actually still be in their own separate, individual worlds.

As a presenter, you're competing for audience *mindshare.* You only have a few seconds to do this and to win their full mindshare. Otherwise, their primary focus will be on their own thoughts. I can't emphasize this enough: it has to happen almost instantly. Even if you were to capture their attention 10 or 15 minutes into your presentation, you would've wasted those first 10 or 15 minutes, and you can't afford to do that. In truth, it's very seldom that a presenter can get the full attention of an audience later in the presentation. It tends to happen right away, or not at all.

So, the question becomes, how do I capture their full attention right away? How do I set up that more compelling reality? You do it with what I call your statement of intent. These are the first few words out of your mouth, and they're designed to let the audience know what you have for them, what they'll get from listening to you, and what benefit it holds for them. The two most important parts of your presentation are the beginning, and the end. These are also the two parts presenters pay the least amount of attention to when they prepare their presentations. Of all the presenters and presentations I've coached, I feel comfortable saying that 98 percent of them put all their attention on the main body of the presentation. Presenters seldom actually start a presentation, they just sort of flow into a beginning. The same thing happens at the end. They don't really finish, they just sort of stop. What's behind these habits are two mistaken assumptions. The first is that the presentation is essentially informational. It's not. Information is just the vehicle for the change that you want to occur. The second assumption is that, at the moment you're presenting, you and the audience automatically share the same context. You don't. If you want to make sure that you and your audience are sharing the same context, you have to state what that context is; you have to set up the common intent and the common context. Assuming that you and the audience share the same context before you've set up that context is exactly like flying to some remote spot halfway around the world, and assuming that the people you encounter will speak your language, with your accent, and know instantly why you've come to see them. Don't be fooled into thinking that because the audience have chosen to be there and they already know the subject matter of your presentation, you automatically share a common context. It just isn't the case. The assumption that presenter and audience automatically share a common context is extremely common, and accounts for the less than optimal results of many presentations.

CHAPTER 8:

Statement of Intent and Common Context

Think of it like this. You go to a vending machine to get a drink, because it's hot, and you're thirsty. The vending machine is the old kind where, after you put your money in, an empty cup appears, and then the drink that you've picked is poured into it. Think of the cup as the context, and the drink as the content of your presentation. What would happen if the drink came down first, then the cup appeared? (This happened to me once.) You would've received exactly the same thing as if the cup appeared first, but because the events happened in the wrong order, you wouldn't have been able to drink whatever it was you paid for. If you give the audience a contextual statement right at the beginning, they'll be able to *drink* whatever it is that you're giving them, and that's the whole point, isn't it?

The contextual statement, (the cup in the analogy I've just used) is the most important part of your presentation. This, and the conclusion, are the only parts of a presentation that I recommend memorizing. Without the contextual statement of intent, you're giving your audience no opportunity to come into your reality, no matter how interesting or compelling that reality may seem to you. Because the first few seconds of being in front of an audience tend to be the most difficult for most people, memorizing your contextual statement, which only has to be one or two sentences long, provides you with a stable platform from which to start. Knowing exactly how you're going to start can be a great source of reassurance. After that, you'll be more willing to fly on your own. I'm not a fan of memorizing scripts; it usually doesn't work. Memorization drains the life out of you, and out of the material you're presenting. There are very few people who can deliver a memorized script and make it sound like the words are just occurring to them, and they tend to be highly trained actors. I keep saying that audiences are very smart on an unconscious level, and this is one of the areas where they're particularly smart. They're almost sure to know if you've memorized the script, and it will make them feel cheated, for several reasons. The first is that they'll get the impression that you aren't sharing the real you with them, that you're essentially hiding from them, which makes it harder for them to trust you. It also creates a temporal disjunction: they know you're not sharing the same present moment with them. You're giving them a version of life that's already happened. The last reason is that when they know you're delivering a memorized script, they'll no longer feel they're part of a creative process, and they'll tend to disengage from you. They need to feel like they're part of what's going on, just like you would if you were in the audience. Memorization is a false security blanket. It might make you feel like you're safe and secure, but it will make the audience feel like you're not really there with them, like you've sent a cardboard cutout of yourself instead of actually appearing before them. Everything I've just said about memorization and how it makes an audience feel cheated is also true of reading a speech to an audience. They don't want you to read to them, they want you to talk to them, to connect with them. Reading a script to an audience is a guarantee that *you* and *they* will never become *we*. You may believe that just talking to an audience without memorization and without reading to them seems too frightening. I understand your concern, but don't worry, we'll deal with that.

The first words out of your mouth are the most important part of a presentation. This is where you'll either capture the full *mindshare* of the audience and ignite their imaginations, or where you'll signal them that they have no reason to come into your reality. Remember, you only have a few seconds to do this. If you don't get their full attention right at the beginning, you won't get it at all. I've seen presenters hold back their essential message until they're far into their presentations, expecting to win over the audience at the last minute. At that point, it's too late; you've lost them because you haven't given them the signal that you have something they need. The first words out of your mouth, your *statement of intent* are not only the most important part of your presentation; they can also be the hardest part of the presentation to craft. (Once you get used to doing it, it's not hard.) For that reason, people tend to pay very little attention to their opening, and instead move directly to *what they're going to say*. The only part of a presentation presenters pay less attention to than the opening is the closing. Coincidentally, this is the second most important part of a presentation.

Let's spend a little time talking about crafting the sort of opening statement, or statement of intent, designed to create a reality more compelling than the one already in the minds of your audience. Compelling opening statements are bold, direct, and simple. Tell them what you have for them, and what it has to do with them. The following are several examples:

"Fifteen minutes from now, I expect that you'll have a completely different view of X. In addition, I predict that when you encounter X, you'll react in a way that will surprise you." (In this opening, you're setting up a specific expectation, and making a promise.)

"Twenty-five years ago, the balloon I was flying in exploded. All of us who were passengers fell two thousand feet into a field that had just been plowed. This is what happened, and how I survived." (This really happened to a friend of mine. It sets up a compelling reality and makes you want to know more, doesn't it?)

"I'm about to share with you a business model so much at odds with the way we've operated up to now that it will seem completely counterintuitive to you. When I'm done, I'll check in with you and see if you've traveled the same distance I have in terms of how you believe we need to be operating in the future. If I've convinced you, I'm going to ask that we re-allocate funds immediately to implement this." (In these three sentences this presenter has set high stakes, and a clear expectation for action from the audience. Chances are high that the audience will be listening carefully.)

This opening moment is where a presenter's shyness, self consciousness, and hesitancy are most likely to appear. This is the moment you're confronted with the fact that you're standing in front of an audience, and they're expecting you to start talking. For most presenters, it's a shocking moment. Presenters sometimes go completely blank as they step in front of an audience. For that reason, it's absolutely critical that you know exactly what your opening statement is going to be. This, and the closing statement are the only parts of a presentation that should be memorized. See if this situation sounds familiar: you think you know what you're going to say, you've rehearsed your presentation, it feels great, you think you know how the presentation is going to go, and that everything is going to be OK. Then the moment comes when you have to stand and deliver, and you have absolutely no idea how to begin or what you're doing, and you either go totally blank, or are so off balance that you make a weak start. This may have happened to you sometime. It's happened to most of us. Knowing exactly how you're going to start, and knowing the words you're going to say can be a great source of reassurance at the moment you may need it most. (Incidentally, *blanking out* like I've just described is much less likely to happen if you've answered the three questions that we'll be dealing with. If you're clear on your goals, it's much easier to regain your bearings.)

Concentrate on connecting with as many eyes in the audience as you possibly can as soon as you start speaking. Your intention as you say those first words should be "Are you getting this? Because our connection and your comprehension are the only things that matter right now." Once you get used to making eye contact, and you'll get used to it very quickly, it becomes the greatest source of reassurance. It's a reminder that you're talking to individual human beings, not to a big, scary monster. Regarding the audience as a monolithic unit creates a great deal of fear. They are a group of individuals who just happen to be in the same place at the same time, and who are waiting for you to guide them. This second point is really important. The audience expects to be taken somewhere by you. You are their guide, and audiences respond to this sort of guidance with relief and gratitude. They relax when you demonstrate, through your connection with them and the sureness of your intention, that you're going to take care of them.

As an example, imagine two buses parked side by side. The driver of the first says, "My bus will be leaving in 15 minutes." The driver of the second bus says, "My bus will be leaving in 15 minutes. We'll be going up through the mountains; we'll gain about five thousand feet in elevation. The weather up there is expected to be extremely clear, and you'll have a view of about a hundred miles, but it'll be a bit cooler than it is here. There's a view of the valley below, and there are hot springs that will be available to you. By the way, I'll be opening the entire top of the bus so that you'll be able to see everything."

Which bus are you more likely to get on? The first driver told you nothing but his departure time. The second driver gave you a graphic preview of the experience you could expect. The first gave you nothing to anticipate, the second set up a very specific set of expectations. Your job as a presenter is to build a specific set of expectations. People like to know where they're going before they get on your bus. Give them that satisfaction, and they'll be willing to enter into your reality.

Once you've shared your statement of intent, you've given the audience the chance to come into your reality, and you've set a context for your presentation. Context is a funny thing though; the best *context setting* involves establishing a consensual context. By that I mean a context that's a collaboration between your context, and the context (or contexts) of the audience. This is when you and the audience really become *we* instead of *me* and *them*. Becoming *we* puts you in the strongest possible position as a presenter. It allows you to be seen as *one of us* by the audience, which allows them to be fully open to you and to your message. One of the best ways to set up this joint context, or consensual context, is by asking questions. Sometimes, you can get most of the information you need about the audience beforehand, during your preparation. Even if you're able to get information before the fact, there might be questions that you feel compelled to ask.

I often ask some sort of questions at the beginning of my presentation, usually right after my statement of intent, though in some situations, I may do it even before I state my intentions. When I'm teaching presentation skills to a class, the first question I ask might be, "How many of you have any fear connected with the idea of presenting to an audience?" Or I might say, "If I invited each one of you up here to give a presentation right this minute about something you know really well, how willing would you be to do it?" A question like one of these accomplishes several things. It lets the audience know I understand that anxiety about presenting is something most of us deal with. That starts to create a consensual context, or consensual reality, and very quickly transforms us from *me and them* to *we*. It's also likely to be taken by them as another sign of respect, and the answer may provide something which allows me to respond in a way that lets them know this presentation is going to be a living conversation, tailored to their needs and desires.

After I've asked that question, the next thing I do is to raise my hand as a model that a raised hand is the signal I'm looking for. In other words, I've just modeled the behavior that I want from the audience. If no hands go up, I add, "Raise your hand if you've ever been afraid before giving a presentation." If you ask a question of the audience, and give them no indication of how you want them to answer, they can be very shy. They're not entirely sure whether you want them to just start talking, or stand up, or raise their hands, and so they do nothing. What's happening at that moment is that they're afraid of feeling foolish by responding inappropriately, so they do nothing. It can be an unnerving moment for the presenter, and can be avoided by simply giving them a clear signal about what you're looking for. Giving clear signals is a great way to strengthen your relationship with your audience. It's another sign of respect, and they'll unconsciously respond to it that way.

As you start your presentation, it's helpful, in fact, it's essential to remember that the audience wants you to do well. People can lose sight of this very easily, and do themselves a huge disservice by doing so. This is really just a form of projecting your fear outward, and mistaking the uneasiness you might feel for a negative feeling from the audience. Audiences are rarely hostile, and even when they are, they'd rather be entertained than bored. If there is hostility, it's usually from a small percentage of individuals. More often than that, it's from a single person. Commonly, audience hostility actually has nothing to do with the presenter; he or she is just the convenient *target of the moment* on which the unhappy person can vent his or her unhappiness. Make sure to be respectful of such individuals. It is not only the right thing to do, if you return their hostility, in a strange way, you come to *own* it. In other words, the rest of the audience can quickly start to feel that you deserve the hostility being aimed at you. At that point, they're likely to identify with the hostile audience member more than they identify with you. The result of this can be a disaster.

CHAPTER 9:

Goal Setting

I said earlier that most presenters focus on what they're going to tell an audience. In other words, they generate content without really understanding, or without being able to articulate exactly what they want to accomplish with their presentation. If you think you know what you're trying to accomplish with a presentation, there's a simple way to test whether you actually know or not. Describe what you're trying to do in one or two sentences. If you aren't able to do this, you don't really know what you're trying to accomplish, you just think you do. This is the right time to talk about setting the goals for your presentation, because once you're clear about your actual goals (not just what you're going to say, which is very different) the appropriate statement of intent, or contextual statement, will be easy to create. The right time to generate goals for your presentation is before you start to play around with what you're going to say. It should be the first work you do on your presentation. Content will flow from goals; it doesn't work the other way around; goals don't flow from content. The only goals that flow from content will be fuzzy goals that won't give you or your audience what any of you need.

There are three questions I like to use to create goals for a presentation. The questions themselves seem so simple that very often people don't want to bother answering them. The questions only *seem* simple. They can be very difficult to answer until you get used to them. There are a number of advantages to using the three questions. Answering these questions will get you focused almost instantly, and will cut your preparation time, probably by half or more. If you use these questions, you'll save a tremendous amount of time. If you resist using them, you'll waste a tremendous amount of time. The choice is yours, and is a simple one. What's your time worth? I understand you may be resistant to taking the time and effort to answer these questions; I've seen this resistance from hundreds of private and corporate clients. I also understand that once you get used to using the three questions, you'll think of them as a valuable tool for getting focused and saving time. I'd like to help you save time, since it seems most of us feel we have too little of it.

These are the questions. The first is (and this one is the most difficult to answer) "What do I want to walk away from this presentation with that I didn't have before I gave it?" I know that this sounds simple, but almost every one of the hundreds of clients I've taught this to starts their answer by saying "I want the audience to..." We'll deal with the audience in the second question. For now, we're talking about what *you* want, so the only pronouns you get to use in this answer are *I* and *me*. There are two purposes to answering this first question. The first is to give you a benchmark against which to judge your progress as a presenter, and to hold yourself accountable for the particular areas where you feel you need to strengthen your presentational skill. You can always strengthen it, no matter how good you are. The second purpose is to give you a personal goal independent of the approval of your audience. If an audience has the impression you're there only for their approval (and this is another of those things audiences are very smart about) you're guaranteed not to get that approval. Having an independent, personal reason for giving a presentation strengthens you both in your own mind, and in the minds of the audience.

I'll give you examples of useful answers to that first question. A good way to start is with the words "I want to walk away feeling..." If you begin this way, you're talking about your personal assessment, not the assessment of someone else. Don't be afraid to be selfish with this answer. You're giving this presentation at least as much for yourself as you are for the audience. You must want something out of the presentation, or you wouldn't be giving it. I said that this question is partly designed to give you a benchmark against which to judge your progress as a presenter, so this is a chance to work on areas of your presentational ability you feel need strengthening. For example, if you had the habit of going too fast and having the feeling of not being in command of your pace, an answer might be "I want to walk away feeling that I took my time and was in complete command of the time I had." If you wanted to work on feeling more authoritative in front of an audience, you might say "I want to walk away feeling I claimed the authority that's my due." If you've ever found yourself in front of an audience who seemed to be on the verge of falling asleep (this often happens in presentations given right after lunch or at the end of a long day) your answer might be "I want to walk away feeling that I was able to generate a high energy level and maintain it throughout my presentation." *State your intention clearly and succinctly.* Assumptions are always an obstacle to clarity. You've got to know what you want out of giving your presentation. If you can't say it simply, *you don't know it.*

Answering this question allows you to take charge of whatever issue you want to work on. By identifying the issues specifically and knowing exactly what you want the outcome to be, you have a good chance of getting what you want. The alternative is to hope for the best and take your chances. That usually doesn't work very well.

Answering the first question might strike you as being a little *touchy-feely.* I understand completely. On the other hand, it's a concrete way of taking charge of some of the fears you have about being in front of an audience. Most of us have some amount of that kind of fear, even if we're good at hiding it from ourselves and from others. I'd rather have you deal with fear actively and productively than to deny the existence of that fear and hope circumstances don't reveal it. The examples I've just given are real, but somewhat generic. As you practice this question, you'll be able to come up with examples specific to you, and specific to the particular presentation you're giving. There's no *one size fits all* answer to this question. The answer will change constantly, depending on your development as a presenter (and by the way, you can learn something from every presentation you ever give. I still do.) The answer will also change depending on the specific nature of each presentation. Always remember to debrief yourself after a presentation and assess whether or not you achieved this goal. If you made any progress at all, give yourself credit. That becomes your new benchmark. Determine to hold yourself responsible to go beyond that new benchmark next time you present.

The second question is generally a little easier to answer, but like the first is not as simple as it looks. You've just talked about what you want to walk away with. Now we're going to think about the audience. The second question is, "What do I want the audience to walk away with that they didn't have when they came into the room?" You should be able to answer this question in one sentence, two at the most. If you're not able to do this, you're not clear on what your purpose is. If you know what you're there for, you'll be able to state it concisely.

In one of the corporations where I've done one-on-one coaching, the man who headed the organization was famous for posing a challenge to presenters who came to his office to give him presentations. Before the presenter could even start, he'd say to the person, "Show me your best slide." Most presenters were completely shaken by this challenge. Afterward, I'd say to them, "Let's decode what he was really saying. He wanted to know if you knew your story in a few words. All he wanted was proof you weren't going to waste his time." His method may have been heavy-handed, but he was able to separate those who knew their story and their purpose from those who didn't.

A common answer from people just learning to use this question starts out "I want them to understand." That may be true, but it doesn't go far enough. You want much more than understanding from your audience. What you really want is for them to feel the same levels of passion and commitment that you feel. If all you're aiming for is audience understanding, that's going to be all you get, and it's not enough. "To understand" is a passive state. Your time and the audience's time are much too valuable to be wasted on passivity. If a presenter stood before you and said, "I'll give you a choice. You can feel passive about what I'm going to present to you, or you can feel passionate about what I'm going to present," which would you pick?

Almost everyone would say that they'd rather feel passionate about a presentation than feel passive. Passion is life; passivity is merely existence. Just like you, audience members want to feel alive. Give them the chance to feel alive when you're presenting to them. Sharing your passion with the audience engages them in a way that demonstrates your respect both for them and for their time, and audience members love that.

I mentioned running back and forth, jumping up and down and generally making a spectacle of yourself as an indication of passion. That sort of display is really just an imitation of passion, and a bad imitation at that. Real passion takes a more subtle form, but ultimately has a more dramatic effect on the audience. As with a number of the principles that I'll be talking about, the most productive place to concentrate is on your intention to have a passionate connection between you, your material and your audience. To do this, you need to have an active goal, stated in active language. If you were to say, "I want the audience to walk out of this room feeling as committed to this proposal as I am," you'd be providing yourself with the necessary high-octane fuel to really change the audience. You should always think of this second goal in terms of how you want to change the audience's perception or behavior. If you're talking about how you want the audience *to understand,* there's no opportunity for sharing your passion with them, for making a connection with them, or for changing them in any way. That's a waste of your time, and of theirs. Frankly, you deserve more for your effort, and so do the audience members.

Soft, fuzzy, passive goals are a protective device, unconsciously designed to keep the stakes low. The unstated reasoning behind this is something like, "If I have low expectations of myself and of this presentation, I won't be disappointed when I don't achieve them." That sounds pretty self-defeating, doesn't it? A presentation has to be seen in terms of what you want to accomplish and what you have to gain, not in terms of what you might lose.

Stating your goals actively and clearly is more than just a semantic exercise; it's crafting a blueprint for what you want to build. I said earlier that I'm accustomed to experiencing strong resistance when I suggest presenters spend time answering these questions. I understand it's tempting to want to jump right in to thinking about what you're going to say, what you want to tell the audience. I understand it's natural to think you know what you're talking about, that you already have a sense of what you want to do with your presentation. Having said that, being able to state what you're there to accomplish will make you infinitely stronger and better prepared than going straight into what you're going to say, or how you're going to say it. I've already said that it will cut your preparation time by getting you focused on what you're trying to accomplish, instead of focusing on what you're going to say without a clearly defined goal. There's another benefit to answering these questions before you start crafting what you're going to say. Before you give a presentation, you probably have an image in your mind of how your presentation is going to go. It's very seldom this image is accurate, because it's impossible to factor in the unknown elements which are always a big part of the mix. Something will always be different than you anticipated, and the trick is to be ready to respond as the situation unfolds. Whatever picture you have in your mind about how your presentation is going to go, the reality will be different from your picture. Plan on that in advance, because it's an absolute. Plan on it ahead of time, and you won't be shocked when unanticipated events occur. If your preparation has been based on *what you're going to say,* you can be badly tripped up when things go differently than you'd expected. If you plan properly by answering the three questions, you'll be better equipped to respond to whatever surprises pop up. In other words, your presentation will have infinite flexibility built into it. A presentation is never about perfection, it's always about how you recover from the surprises that happen, and we'll go into that in greater detail a bit later.

Unanticipated occurrences during a presentation can actually work in your favor, if you deal with them properly. When the power goes out, when you have difficulties with your computer, when the presentation that was going to be 45 minutes is suddenly shortened to 5 minutes, you can use those events to strengthen your connection with the audience. When the audience sees you respond to unplanned events, adapt, and keep going, several things happen. They're reminded that you're a live human being responding to life as it unfolds (instead of being an automaton presenting a rehearsed imitation of life, with all the *juice* sucked out of it). That reinforces their sense that they're participants in the presentation, not merely observers; so it boosts their sense of engagement with you, the presenter. It also reminds them that you know what you're there to achieve, that you know what you want for them, and from them, and that nothing is going to stop you from reaching your goal. In addition, on an unconscious level, they'll read your ability to adapt as a sign of respect for them, which further strengthens your connection to them. When you respond to an unplanned event, and recover from it, it can be to your advantage. The sort of recovery from surprise events that I'm talking about is very difficult to pull off, if when you planned your presentation, you focused only on what you were going to say and how you were going to say it. There's no margin for error or for the unexpected when you build a presentation that way. It's like building a house without a blueprint. You may know where you want to put the entrance, the kitchen, and the bedrooms. You may know how many bathrooms you want, and where they're going to be in relation to the other rooms, but this level of planning is inadequate if you expect to physically build a house.

Answering the three questions gives you an infinitely flexible and adaptable blueprint. I'm making a big point about this because, as I said before, I've seen resistance from hundreds of people who are convinced that answering the questions is a waste of their time. It's only when they've used the questions that they become converts, and ironically, those whose resistance has been strongest become the most avid converts.

So let's summarize the most effective way to answer the second question, "What do I want them to walk away with?" It should be a single sentence, two at the most, and it should be stated as actively as you possible can, with words like *convinced, converted, committed, passionately,* and so on. Words like *understand, know, and learn* are low stakes, passive verbs and give you nothing to aim for. In fact, they keep you disconnected from your audience.

The third question is "What do I want them to do as a consequence of having heard me?" In other words, "what specific action do I want them to take?" I said earlier that assumptions are always an obstacle to clarity. The third question deals with an area that's ripe for assumption. Depending on the nature of the presentation you're giving, the answer to this question can be wildly obvious. In other situations, it can be more difficult to identify. In either case, it's crucial that you be able to state how you want to change the audience's behavior, or change their perception. Answers to the third question are usually simple and straightforward. "I want them to approve and allocate the funding for my proposal." "I want them to see mentally disabled people as their equals." "I want them to take full advantage of the resources I've outlined for them." Though these answers can seem obvious, if you can't state them this clearly, you don't really know what the stakes are for your presentation. Write out the answers to all three of the questions. Do it when you first start to think about the presentation. Fight the temptation to start generating *what you're going to say.*

I've dealt with the three questions early on because I want to make sure you start to incorporate them into your thinking about giving presentations. This is the most productive place to start whenever you're putting together a presentation. There's still value to answering the questions later on in the process, but the later you answer them in your preparation, the more time you will have wasted. Finally, the most important value of answering these questions is that they help to take your focus away from self-consciousness and connect you to your goals and to the audience.

Before we finish talking about goals, I have a true story to share that illustrates the value of answering the three questions, especially in terms of how they equip you to be infinitely flexible and adaptable to changing circumstances. I was once given the task of helping set up a decision-making review board in the drug development wing of a pharmaceutical company. It was established with the goal of being a *stage gate* committee, in other words, the committee gave the go-ahead for drugs under development to go from one very clearly defined stage of development to the next. Because drugs are the most heavily regulated product made, this had to be done within extremely strict guidelines. I performed several functions: I helped insure that whenever one of the potential product development teams made a presentation to the committee, they could be guaranteed of walking away from the meeting with a decision in hand. I made it clear to the committee members that the reputation of the committee depended on its ability to make clear, timely decisions. I was also in the unusual position of helping streamline and strengthen the presentations delivered to the committee by development team members. So I helped fashion the presentations, and then, as a non-voting member of the committee, I watched the presentations being given.

In one meeting, there were severe complications with one of the products being developed, and that particular issue took up most of the all-day meeting, completely upsetting the agenda. At the end of the meeting, we made time to see one of the scheduled presentations (all of the others had to be rescheduled). This particular product was also having serious complications (which are very common for drugs in development) and a decision had to be made that day. The man who was going to present had been given forty-five minutes for his presentation. I had run through his presentation with him several times, and it was very strong. It presented a series of intricate issues, and forty-five minutes was an appropriate amount of time. There was no *fat* in the presentation; it had been trimmed down to essentials. But it was the end of the day, people were tired, and had planes to catch. The president of the company, who was chairman of the committee, asked the presenter, who was already standing at the front of the conference room, ready to go, if he could give his presentation in five minutes instead of forty-five. "No," the presenter said, "I can do it in three minutes, with one slide." He did just that, he got his decision, the committee actually applauded, and everyone went away happy. He was able to achieve what seemed to be a miracle partly because when we rehearsed, I asked him the three questions, and the presentation was crafted from the answers. He was completely clear and focused on what he wanted to accomplish, not on what he was going to say. So, when the situation threatened to turn him upside down, he instantly found his balance.

If you've answered the three questions, you'll have an ironclad sense of intent; if you haven't answered them, you're leaving this to chance. Remember what I said earlier about how presenters spent too much time focusing on uncontrollable elements and not enough time on controllable ones? Your goals represent controllable elements. Spend plenty of time crafting them properly. This is the most valuable investment you can make in your presentation.

CHAPTER 10:

Being Seen and Heard

Your next obligations to the audience are to be seen, and to be heard. Sounds silly, right? There are usually lights, if necessary, and there's often a microphone, if you're talking to a crowd of any size. I'm taking the time to mention these two obligations, being seen, and being heard, because I can't count the number of times I've watched people stand in the darkest corner of the stage, or part of the room where they're expected to present, and speak so softly that nobody could really hear them. If there are lights, (especially if a podium or lectern isn't being used) find the brightest spot, in other words, the spot where the light in your face is brightest, and feels warmest. If you have any doubt that you can be seen by the audience, just ask, "Can everyone see me?" If you get no response, address your question to a specific corner of the room, "Can you see me back there in the corner?" If the audience can't see your eyes, if they can't see the expressions on your face, they have no reason to trust you, and likely, they won't. Then we're back to no trust, and so no connection, no openness, no passage of information, and no opportunity to change their minds or bring them to a new place. Unfortunately, many conference rooms are set up so that all the light is focused where the PowerPoint images will appear, instead of where it belongs, on the face of the presenter. Often, you'll have to try to adjust to this less-than-ideal situation. If people can't see you, try to move to where they can see you, or ask if there's any way to make the lights brighter. If nothing can be done, acknowledge (don't complain, just acknowledge) that it's not an ideal situation, and why it isn't ideal, then let them know that you'll do everything you can to compensate, because you have something for them they need, or can use. Then just move on, and focus on making the strongest contact with the audience you possibly can.

The audience not being able to hear you is much more common than their not being able to see you. In fact, speaking too softly is an epidemic. Few people have an idea of how loud they need to be, even in a small room, with a small audience. Inadequate volume is a result of several factors. Unless you've been trained to be aware of how much volume you need to generate, and have an objective view of how loud your voice actually is, in the anxiety-producing circumstances of a presentation, your volume will be less than it is in everyday circumstances, and will be too low. When we hear our own voices, we hear them amplified by a really wonderful resonator; the bones in our head. This is why when you hear a recording of your voice, it sounds "tinny" and artificial. "Is that really how I sound?" People often ask when they hear their own recorded voices. So we have a false sense of both what our voices sound like, and how loud they are.

Add to that any sense of fear about presenting, and the volume becomes even lower. This is especially true at the beginning of a presentation, when presenters tend to be most nervous, and just at the point where they're trying to establish their intent, their credibility, and their relationship with the audience; in other words, just when they need to be loudest. Don't worry about *being too loud*. (This is an excuse I often hear when I tell presenters that they can't be heard: "I'm afraid I'll be too loud.") The chance you'll be too loud is small, and even if you are a little loud, at least the audience will hear what you have to offer them. What happens most often when a presenter speaks too softly is that the audience can't hear, and so they miss big important chunks of what's being said. Audience members rarely address this issue; they're too polite, or too unwilling to call attention to themselves. When an audience member does speak up and asks for more volume, the presenter is often surprised, and thrown off. There's no reason to be thrown off; this is information that you need. By the way, if you're asked to talk louder, you have to do it for the rest of the presentation, not just for the next sentence or two, as I commonly see. Just for the record "I can hear myself just fine" has nothing to do with how well the audience can hear you. Volume level has to be regulated for the audience, not for the speaker, unless you're planning to give a presentation to yourself. What usually happens when your volume is too low is that no one says anything, the audience doesn't hear most or all of your presentation, and they stay firmly in their own separate realities, instead of coming into yours, where you need them to be.

Don't ever hesitate to ask the audience if you have any doubt at all about their being able to hear you. "Can everyone hear me?" If you get no answer, don't be afraid to ask in another way. "Anyone having trouble hearing me?" Is my voice loud enough for you to hear?" If you happen to have a soft voice, you could even say, "If my voice gets too soft for you to hear, I'm depending on you to let me know because I really want you to hear me." These are legitimate questions and comments, and will give you information that you absolutely need. Asking them, and responding appropriately to the answers you get is another way of starting to build your relationship with the audience. You're demonstrating another sign of respect for the audience. The only reason you're up there talking is to give them something you have for them, and that they need. Even though they sometimes respond slowly, the audience love to be asked if they're getting what they need.

Don't ever be fooled by the presence of a microphone into thinking that you can speak softly. Unless you have a sound technician assigned to continuously monitoring your volume and compensating for you as needed, you still need to be louder than you think you do. Driving in your car is a great place to practice talking at a volume greater than what you're accustomed to using. You'll start feeling comfortable with more volume very quickly if you practice in your car. If you're worried about looking foolish, don't be; other drivers will just think you're talking on a hands-free phone.

There are a couple of final points about volume. Subconsciously, the audience equates volume with the presenter's level of commitment to what he or she is saying. When I'm working with people in person, I usually do a demonstration when I'm talking about volume.

I get as far away from the person or people in the room as I can and start talking to them, connecting to them as strongly as I can. Because I'm experienced in knowing how much volume I need in particular circumstances, I start by talking at a volume appropriate to the size of the room, the number of people in it (remember; bodies absorb sound) and whatever ambient noise may exist in the room. Then, with exactly the same intention and level of contact, I take my volume as far down as I can, knowing they can still just barely hear me. After talking like this for a minute, I bring my volume back up to what I know is an appropriate level. Then I ask them to describe how committed I appear to them at each of the two levels of volume. Invariably, they tell me that the greater my volume, the greater their sense of my commitment. You want to be able to give your audience every chance to believe and absorb what you're telling them. Volume is one of your most important tools.

Another benefit of adequate volume when you're speaking has to do with what I call *expressive bandwidth*. The more volume you're using, the more variation you have to work with to emphasize the operative words and phrases that you absolutely need the audience to hear. These are the words and phrases without which you won't be able to get your points across to the audience. Expressive band width has a number of physical tools: among them, speeding up and slowing down your flow of words for emphasis, as well as the rise and fall of the *music* of your speech. Along with pace and pitch, one of the most common and useful tools is variation in volume. In normal speech, we vary the degree of volume we use quite a bit. If all you're using is low volume, you're leaving a valuable tool in your tool box.

One final point about volume. I hope you've never had a full-fledged panic attack when you were presenting, and I want to make sure that never happens. A large number of presenters have felt some sense of near-panic, or strong fear. Talking at full volume requires you to breathe more deeply, and to take in more oxygen, than talking in a soft voice does. A common origin of presenter's panic is actually physiological, not emotional or psychological, as most of us would assume. Hypoxia is a condition that happens when the brain isn't getting enough oxygen. When you add a level of fear to hypoxia, panic can happen very quickly. So, talking at full volume not only ensures that the audience will be able to hear you, and that you'll sound committed to what you're saying, it also gets enough oxygen to your brain so that you're less likely to freak out. Experiment with speaking at greater volume. You'll probably find higher volume also frees you up physically, which in turn will help you relax in every sense.

CHAPTER 11:

Establishing the Right Energy in the Room

Your next obligation is to bring the audience to the energy level that you want. Remember, *you* dictate the energy in the room, not the audience. If you adjust your energy to theirs, the results can be disastrous, especially if you're scheduled to speak to them just after lunch, when their blood sugar levels are about to dive, or if you're presenting at the end of the day, when everyone in the room is exhausted. Presenters can feel so defeated by walking into a room full of tired or disengaged people that the presentation is over before it begins. Most of the time, you can't afford to blend into the existing energy in the room. The exception to this is if the energy you want, in other words, engaged, enthusiastic, and attentive, already exists in the room. It's up to you to look for and recognize this energy when it exists. Then all you have to do is ride that wave. If the energy in the room isn't what you want it to be, bring the energy yourself. You have to be bold enough to stand out. After all, you're the center of attention while you're presenting. Claim it; the audience members want you to claim it, and it's yours for the taking.

This is a situation where knowing what you want to accomplish is incredibly important. If you've answered the three questions, you'll be much better equipped to spot any dissonance between what you need to accomplish, and whatever energy existing in the audience (for example, fatigue, distraction, or hostility) might stand in the way of accomplishing your goals. Adopting the energy of the audience is a way to turn yourself into a victim of circumstances. Making yourself into a victim is always self-defeating, and never more so than when you step in front of an audience. Don't expect to automatically get the energy you want from the audience. This is another example of what I talked about when I said, "Give what you want to get in return." In other words, give them the energy that you want from them. If you want them to be energetic, engaged, passionate, and respectful, show them that energy coming from you. Remember that I said they're waiting for a signal from you in terms of how they should respond? This is another example of that expectation on their part. Give them what you want back, and you'll seldom be disappointed. Wait to get it from them, and you'll usually be disappointed. Take charge of that energy before you even start presenting, and be very clear about what you want. That will guide you in terms of what you need to give. (Just to be clear, what I'm talking about is accomplished by intention. This isn't something you say to the audience; it's something you do through intention.)

We're still talking about what's happening at the beginning of your presentation; you're setting things up. Since it's up to you to establish the *rules of engagement* (if you don't, things will happen by chance or default, and they won't necessarily be to your advantage) this is a perfect opportunity for you to acknowledge that people will probably have questions, and how you want to deal with them.

CHAPTER 12:

Taking Questions from the Audience

Ideally, you want to be able to answer questions as they come up, while they're still fresh in people's minds, and before you move on to a different topic. This is ideal for a number of reasons: it allows you to respond *in the moment* so that you are more likely to be able to keep people in your flow and progression. If an audience member has a burning question, and isn't allowed to ask it, that person tends to focus entirely on the question or issue that he wants to have addressed, so until you allow him to ask it, you've lost him. Answering questions as you go makes those asking questions feel respected, as though you're custom fitting the presentation to their needs (which is what you should be doing) and it gives you invaluable information about the level of comprehension coming from your audience members. Finally, it gives you a stronger sense that your presentation is a conversation. (I said this earlier; a presentation is always a conversation, because even when you're doing all the talking, you're still receiving from the audience. You may not be receiving words, but you're receiving information.) Questions are often the part of a presentation that presenters are most comfortable with, so getting to them quickly can be to your advantage.

After the opening statement of intent, I like to say, "Please feel free to ask questions as they come up." In certain circumstances, you might even add "It helps me understand what's important to you, and what you particularly want to hear about." You've just set up the protocol for questions. As I mentioned earlier, the audience like to know what the rules are. They only know if you tell them. Openly stating that questions are okay has another advantage. You may find yourself in a situation where there's a distinct hierarchy in place (for example, a business presentation) and where you may be presenting to people who occupy a higher level than you do. Often, they'll feel entitled to interrupt you with questions. This can be hard to control, given your relative spots on the food chain. By your having given the okay to questions beforehand, you won't look as though you're being steamrolled, and it won't seem that way to you either.

If an audience member asks a question you're not able to answer, don't worry, it's not the end of the world. There are a couple of ways to deal with it. If you don't know, the best route is to simply say, "I don't know." You're not expected to know everything, or to be perfect, and expecting that from yourself sets you up to fail. The audience is human; they know that you are too. If you try to answer without really knowing, chances are the audience will figure out you don't know what you're talking about. You can also say, "I don't know, but I'll find out for you." If you don't know the person asking the question, ask to meet with them after the presentation so that you can get their contact information and follow up with them.

Sometimes, you may not know the answer to a question, but someone else in the audience does. If you think that might be the case, you can say, "I don't know, but there are people here who probably know more than I do. Does anybody know the answer?" It's not important for you *to know everything*. Your being willing to act as a facilitator who gets the answer to a question is just as useful as having the answer yourself. You're in a stronger position by setting yourself up as *the person who wants to find out* than by trying to be *the person who knows everything.*

If a question comes up that deals with an issue you're planning to cover, say something like, "Great question. It's a subject I'll be getting to in just a little while, so if you wouldn't mind, I'm going to ask you to remind me of that question when we get to it, so that I can give it the attention it deserves."

One last point about taking questions. There will be times when questioners are more interested in showing how much they know than in hearing your response to their question. Learn to identify this type of question. Be respectful, but don't let them take over your presentation. Sometimes they'll try to do just that. They may be much more interested in having attention paid to them than to having a question answered. Let them know that you take them and their question seriously, that it deserves more time than you can give to it now, given the limited time you have, and ask them to meet with you afterward. Sometimes, they won't even show up. Sometimes, they will, and you may have to spend some time listening to them, but that's better than having your presentation hijacked.

CHAPTER 13:

Primary Relationship

I want to talk a little about what I call your *primary relationship*. This might seem obvious, but because I see the primary relationship misplaced so often, I'm compelled to be really clear about it. Your primary relationship is with the members of the audience. In other words, it's when you are fully engaged with your audience, making the sort of eye contact that takes in the whole room and lets them know that you both have something for them, and want something from them (their engagement and comprehension.) Your primary relationship isn't with your notes, it isn't with your slides, it isn't with anything else. When presenters focus on anything other than the audience, it's because they're afraid of something, and this is another situation where the audience subconsciously knows the presenter is afraid. The result of their knowing is that they start to withdraw from you because they feel you've withdrawn from them, and they don't like it. They want you to engage them and to engage with them. When a presenter seems to focus on her notes, or slides, or something other than the audience, it comes from a fear that she, the presenter, is less interesting than her slides, or notes. This is a false fear. Even if you have the best slides anyone has every seen, you're still more interesting than your slides, because *you* picked them or created them, and understand their significance and context. You're *always* more interesting than your slides, and it's really important that you realize that and acknowledge it. If you don't believe it, neither will your audience.

The fears that we have when we're in front of an audience are magnifications of fears we have about ourselves in more everyday situations. In everyday situations, the fears can be easy to ignore. In front of an audience, they feel too enormous to be ignored. This particular fear, feeling like you're not interesting enough, is an incredibly common one. The important thing to remember is that the more connected you are to your audience, the more interesting you seem to them. The more connected you are to your audience, the less time you have to think about yourself, and your doubts and fears. Focusing on the fears actually accentuates them. Putting your full attention on the connection you're making with your audience members, on whether or not they seem to be getting what you're saying, and on the goals you want to achieve will make these fears seem to evaporate. If you do this for a while, you'll be surprised to see that you had nothing to be afraid of all along, that it was all an illusion. That can be hard to believe until you experience it. Once you have experienced it, it's like a weight has been lifted off your shoulders, and you never have to carry it again.

Honoring your primary relationship, your relationship with the audience, is what will make you seem interesting. I understand that it might seem counter-intuitive to connect with the thing you fear, your audience. Don't worry if it seems counter-intuitive. Just try it. Lead with the body and the mind will follow.

Obviously, you may have to refer to notes occasionally, or to slides, if you're using them. I say, "if" because in many situations *you don't have to use slides.* If slides really and truly enhance your presentation, fine, use them. If they don't, all they do is to break the connection between you and your audience. Overdone, complicated, unnecessary slides cut you off from your audience and rob you of your most important feedback mechanism; eye contact. If you can do without slides, do without. The best presentations I've ever seen, and the best ones I've ever given, didn't use slides.

If you're using slides, and you have to look at your slide for some reason, to find something on it that you want to emphasize, for example, keep facing the audience. The second you turn your back on them, you're no longer honoring your primary relationship. You've given them the message that they're no longer the most important thing in the room. Remember: they want to feel like they're the most important thing in the room, and when they don't, they have no reason to stay with you, so they go back into their own worlds. When you watch the weather report on TV, there's a reason that the technology exists enabling the weather person to face the camera (the audience, in other words) and draw on the weather map. How often do you ever see a weather person turn away from the camera? Almost never, and if they do, it's only for a split second. You can back right up to the surface (the wall or screen) where your slides are being projected, face the audience, and gesture to what you need them to see. If you need to look at the slide for a moment, just turn your head, don't turn your whole body away from the audience. When you point to something on one of your slides, do it with your hand, not with a laser pointer. There's only one time a laser pointer is of any help to the audience. That's if you have a slide heavy with numbers or data, and you need them to focus on one particular number, or contrast one number or figure to another. Presenters love laser pointers for one simple reason; it gives them something to do with their hands. You can accomplish the same thing by holding a pen. It feels like your hand has a task, and so you don't have to think about it. The best thing to do with your laser pointer is to put it under the wheel of your car, and drive away. You don't need it, it's just another false security blanket; it gives you nothing, and it gives the audience even less, especially when the presenter uses it to make circles around each bullet point. This is a mistake especially when you're nervous, because the laser dot on the screen jumps all over the place, telegraphing your nervousness.

If you're thinking about what to do with your hands, as I just described, your focus is in the wrong place, and you have to get it back to where it belongs, on the audience. Remember, the more you're thinking about yourself, the less you're able to reveal who you really are, and the weaker your connection to your audience. You remain *me* and *them*, never *we* or *us*. The less you're thinking about yourself, the stronger your connection to them, the more interesting you seem, and the more you're able to reveal yourself as someone who can be trusted. You become *us*, and the arbitrary, frightening distinctions of *me* and *them* disappear. That's when you have full access to the hearts and minds of your audience.

If you have to look at your notes, do it as quickly as you can. The easiest and most effective notes are simple words or short phrases that help you keep your flow and serve as reminders of topics you need to cover. Write or print them big enough so that you can instantly focus back and forth between the audience and your notes, otherwise you may panic at not being able to find your place.

Writing out your entire presentation is another false security blanket. Unless you're planning to read it, which is the worst possible choice you can make, you won't be able to find your place when you look down, and you'll panic, and be tempted to read it to them. Audiences hate to have presentations or speeches read to them. (The extremely rare exception, is when a presenter is skilled enough to use a teleprompter to full advantage. The person using the teleprompter shouldn't be the one who judges whether he or she is skilled enough. Never use one of these without having the best objective advice available to you as to your level of skill.) Reading to an audience only proves one thing; that you know how to read, and they already take that for granted. When you read your presentation to them, you make no connection, and so they feel like you're not really there. If you're going to read to them, you might as well record it in advance, and send a full-size cardboard cut-out of yourself instead of physically being there. The effect will be exactly the same. Reading to the audience does them as huge injustice; it robs them of your actual presence and connection to them. It does you as the presenter an equally huge injustice, because it makes you appear to be much less than you are. The only benefit to reading is that it gives you a completely illusory feeling of safety.

Every time you break your primary relationship with the audience, they have the chance to migrate back into their own separate realities, and some of them will. The more time you spend in eye contact with them, the stronger the message becomes that you have something important for them, and that you're committed to getting it across to them.

Honoring your primary relationship, and avoiding the distractions of slides, notes, and anything else that gets in the way of your connection to your audience, is one of the best ways to ensure you'll achieve the goals you've set up for your presentation. If for any reason, you have to *leave* your audience for a moment, get back to them as quickly as you possibly can.

Another part of your primary relationship with the audience has to do with listening. I said earlier that a presentation is always a conversation. You may be doing all or most of the talking, but it's still a conversation in the sense that it's an exchange. Because you'll be doing most of the talking, you have to listen even more carefully than you do in a more conventional conversation. You should be paying close attention to how attentive they are, to what points they really seem to respond to, and whether or not they're *getting it*. The sort of listening you have to employ is what's called *deep listening*. Though it includes listening with your ears, it's much more than that. When you're the one talking, you also have *to listen with your eyes*, and with all your senses, particularly your intuitive senses. The audience is transmitting a tremendous amount of non-verbal information to you. It's your responsibility to pick up as much of that information as you possibly can, and you'll need all your senses in order to do that. This is one of the elements of a presenter's relationship with the audience that's most often ignored, and always at the expense of the presenter and his presentation. The sort of listening I'm describing allows you to *take the temperature* of your audience continuously, throughout your presentation. If at any point you need more information about whether or not you're getting through to them than you're able to get by listening, just ask. Comments like, "Does that make sense?" Or, "Does anyone feel like they need to hear more about that? Because I'll be happy to explain it in a different way if anyone is unclear," go a long way toward making sure that the audience is *with you*. Sometimes, the non-verbal information they're giving you isn't enough, and you have to ask them. As I said before, the audience love to be asked if something makes sense to them, or if they need to hear more about it, or need clarification, or have questions about a specific point. You have to know, in real time, what they need, so that you can give it to them. Give them what they want, and you're much more likely to get what you want in return.

One last point about the primary relationship. If you honor your primary relationship by fully engaging with your audience at all times, by being respectful of them, by letting them know you have something for them, and need something from them, and by really listening to them, you make the presentation *about them*. Unless it's about them, they're not really interested, and not really there. Make it about them, and they'll find you and your material interesting.

CHAPTER 14:

Story, Flow, and Transitions

You have a story to tell or you wouldn't be preparing to stand in front of an audience and give a presentation. You may not think of your presentation as a story, but it will be to your advantage to start doing so. Very simply, this is how human beings like to get information. People remember stories more easily than they remember facts. Think of a story as an organizing principle around which information can be wound, or as a box to hold information. A story humanizes information and reveals it as having something to do with our lives. Our brains gravitate to stories, and we remember them with ease. Because they engage the imagination of the listener, stories allow us to insert ourselves into them in a way that facts don't. Remember when I talked about needing to grab an audience on both an intellectual level and an emotional level? This is what a story does. In other words, we can easily imagine stories happening to us. Daniel Pink, in his excellent *A Whole New Mind* refers to story as "content enriched by context." Take advantage of this: your audience is looking for a story. Give them one, and you'll maximize the chance they'll be open to what you have for them.

You probably won't be starting your presentation with, "Once upon a time..." and you don't need to. A story is a combination of information and emotional context. The combination may be why it's easy to retain content presented as a story. There will be emotion in your story as long as you're clear on why you're telling it; what it has to do with the audience, and why it's important to you.

A successful story has a flow to it. One thing leads to another, out of which emerges the next. Stories connect pieces of information. I've already made my aversion to slides well known, but because it's likely you'll be using slides of some sort, it's vital that one slide link to the next. If they do, you're well on your way to having a story. If they don't, all you have is a pile of content the audience will be unable to process. The most important thing for you to know about each slide is how it links to the next, and your slides should be set up so they flow this way. No matter how logically you think they may be arranged, it's up to you to make this connection for the audience. What's seems logical to you won't necessarily be obvious to them. You're the facilitator of your story, and you have to tell the audience how one slide links to the next. Being able to provide these verbal transitions becomes the glue that holds your story together. There are additional benefits to having good linkage between your slides: the audience gets the impression that they're seeing and hearing your story as it's being created. Finally, good linkage between slides creates the impression the story is coming from you, not from your slides, which contributes to their sense of how commanding a presenter you are.

Here are several examples of phrases I've used or heard used to link one slide to the next:

"Earlier I mentioned three reasons this program is a sound investment. Let's take a look at them."

"Everything I've said up to now is an expression of how we've assumed our environment to be. What I'm about to show you now sweeps a number of those assumptions away.

"The amount of time we spend sleeping is considered by many of us to be wasted time. The only purpose of sleep we're sure of is that it gives our brains an opportunity to 'flush' information we don't need. This next slide will give you some idea of what actually might be going on in your mind when you're asleep."

"Which leads us directly to my next point." (I like simple and effective transitions like this one.)

"On the other hand" (This is a great transition when one point of view has been presented and another is about to be revealed. If you use this, put the slide up first, so the audience can see you're about to give them a completely different point of view, then introduce it with, "On the other hand").

As you put up each new slide, avoid the temptation to read the title, which creates the impression that the information on the slide is coming from the slide, instead of from you. *You are the source of information;* the slides are only an enhancement. The last thing the audience wants to believe is that your information is coming from the slides, instead of from you. This tends to make you look like the teacher who is only one lesson ahead of his students. If you fall into this trap, you're throwing away your credibility, and there's no reason to do that.

CHAPTER 15:

The Illusion of Perfection

The most important thing to understand about perfection in a presentation is that it doesn't exist. The small imperfections are what make it human, and as a result, make it much more interesting to the humans who will be watching or listening to it. This is the difference between something that's been made by hand, and something that's been mass produced by machine. The two things look and feel very different from one another. The one made by hand contains a humanity that the one made by machine can never have. Since you're not a machine, you don't want to appear to be one; you want your humanity to show. Humans aren't perfect. The audience don't expect you to be perfect. Don't put that unreasonable expectation on yourself.

Presentations aren't about perfection; they're about recovering from the small "mistakes" and surprises that invariably come up in any and every presentation. That sort of recovery serves multiple purposes: It reminds the audience that what is happening on the stage, in front of their eyes, is *real life* passing before them; it isn't a rehearsed imitation of life. This makes them feel they're part of the creative process going on in front of them, and they really want to feel they're part of it. That's what makes it possible for them *to own the presentation.* When a mistake or a surprise happens, and the members of the audience see the presenter recover from that surprise, it reminds them that nothing is going to stop the presenter from achieving her goal of getting through to them. I'm sure you've seen a runner stumble in a foot race, and go all the way down to the ground. What happens when the runner gets up as quickly as she can and starts running again? The crowd goes wild and shows great support for the determination of that runner. They root for the runner much more than if she hadn't fallen. Mistakes or surprises can actually work to your advantage, if you use them to make clear that your intention is ironclad, that nothing is going to stop you. The audience will like you even more for it and feel more connected to you than if the mistake or surprise didn't happen.

Here's a reminder about something you can plan on in every presentation you'll give for the rest of your life: However you think it will go, it won't. There'll always be surprises, and there'll always be mistakes. There's no reason to be disappointed by either one, or to feel you've failed. The only failure is failing to recover from the un-planned event. Technical failures are the most common unplanned events. Your computer won't *sync* with the projector, the projector won't work, you end up with the wrong version of your slides, or the electricity for the whole building goes out. You've either seen all of these possibilities, or they've happened to you. It simply doesn't mat-ter. None of it matters if you know your goals and have done basic preparation. If all the technical aspects of your presentation fail, you can still just talk to the audience. They won't care about technical dif-ficulties if you don't. Usually, they'd rather just be talked to anyway, as long as you really strive to make a connection with them and get through to them. If that intention on your part is strong, none of the rest of it matters. Even if you forget your notes, you can still recover from it. When something goes wrong, the most important thing for you to do is to acknowledge it. The audience will turn on you if they sense that something has happened and you're pretending that it hasn't happened. Acknowledge whatever happens. Chances are that they've seen it before you have. In other words, If you can't fix it, feature it. Turn it to your advantage. Even in the example of discovering you've forgotten your notes (which I've done) all you have to do is admit it. "I just discovered I've forgotten my notes, but what I have to say to you is important enough that I'm just going to talk to you." The worst thing you can do is to apologize for a mistake. Apologizing to an audience for something completely out of your control is the same as bending over, grabbing the edge of the rug, and pulling it out from under your-self. Acknowledging a mistake or surprise and apologizing for it are two different things. Acknowledge it, and keep going. The exception to this is if you've somehow offended the audience, or aren't able to deliver on a particular promise that you've made, such as giving them handouts, or copies of your book. In those situations, of course you have to apologize. Do it sincerely, and move on.

I'll give you an example of something going wrong that could easily have been a presenter's nightmare. I was presenting to the top managers of a large medical device company (they make implants, catheters, stents, things that are inserted into the body during surgery.) There were several hundred people in the audience. I was talking about how important it is to always be mindful that the products they developed and manufactured actually ended up in patients who could easily have been their family members. It's easy for people to lose sight of the effect a product can have on a patient or customer when they have no direct contact with those patients and customers. As an example, I was talking about my having worked with a drug development team in a pharmaceutical company. The product they were developing was a transdermal patch designed to deliver a dose of heavy pain medication. One of the patch's primary uses was to keep dying patients out of pain. I worked with this team for several years, during which time the product was approved by the Food and Drug Administration, and then launched and marketed.

The patch was completely theoretical to me. Then, when my father was dying, and in a great deal of pain, he was given the patch that I'd been so familiar with on a theoretical level. My father had only died a year or so earlier, but as I told the story, I was probably even more surprised than the audience to find that I was crying, and all of a sudden couldn't talk. I could hardly pretend it wasn't happening, and I had to do something fast, so I let myself start laughing, and said something like, "If this ever happens to you, and you start crying in public, just start laughing at the same time and no one will mind." I instantly diffused the situation. I made it about all of us, instead of about me, and I went right on with my presentation. It worked perfectly. Showing you're able to laugh at yourself will always endear you to an audience. You're showing them your humanity and humility. The same is true if you make a mistake, or say the wrong word. Acknowledge your mistake. You don't have to say, "Oh, I just made a mistake." Just don't pretend it didn't happen. If you're able to laugh at yourself, all the better. Then pick up where you left off, and continue. The same is true if you happen to stumble on a word or words, or you happen to say the wrong word. I recently heard a very gifted speaker say "abdonimable" when he meant to say "abominable." He corrected himself, and moved on. Nobody cared. They stayed right with him. Sometimes, you simply can't wrap your mouth around what you're trying to say, and it comes out a jumble of words, or in the wrong order. When this happens to me, I can't resist the chance to parody myself. I intentionally make an even bigger mess of it before I correct myself. I've found that doing that is a great way to clear my mouth and really put the mistake behind me. (I love to laugh, like most people do, and I'm not one to waste a good laugh just because I'm the butt of it.) If you can't fix it, feature it. Mistakes are always an opportunity to show your humanity, your humility, and your ability to laugh at yourself. They show that you're a living, breathing, mortal human, just like the members of the audience. Mistakes can strengthen your connection to the audience. Mistakes are not your enemies; they're friends that can increase your connection to your audience, if you choose to see them that way. Besides, they're inevitable. Why not use them to your advantage? Don't worry about *getting it right*. Focus on letting out what you want to share with your audience, and you'll be fine.

CHAPTER 16:

Brevity

Your presentation should always be organized around this principle: *How little can I tell them?* If members of an audience want to know more than you've told them, they can always ask for it. It's much harder for them to let you know that you're telling them too much. Overwhelming an audience by telling them too much sends them right back into their own personal realities, and disconnects them from the common, consensual reality that you're trying to set up and maintain. There are multiple reasons for telling an audience too much, for going on too long. The most common have to do with the presenter feeling an unnecessary need to prove his or her expertise, and the mistaken notion that talking for a long time, and really cramming everything a presenter knows into the presentation will secure the approval of the audience. This is an example of asking for the approval of the audience, and can be summed up by the phrase, "Tell me I'm doing OK. Tell me that you think I know what I'm talking about." The audience members don't want to be asked for approval. That suggests to them a lack of confidence on the part of the presenter, and plants the thought that maybe he doesn't know what he claims to know. The audience would always rather be told than asked. (The exception to this is asking the audience for information they have and the presenter doesn't. For example, "How many of you have been in your current position for more than two years?" That sort of asking is perfectly fine.) Asking for approval through the attitude you transmit insures that you'll never get that approval.

If your tone suggests to them that you're asking for approval or validation, they'll withhold it. "If this presenter doesn't believe in herself, why should I believe in her?" Tell them, don't ask them. You're probably giving the presentation because it's been established that you know more about the subject than anyone else in the room, or that you have a particular perspective on the subject than no one else has. (If others in the room know more than you do, acknowledge it with something like, "A number of you have a deeper knowledge about X than I do. I may call on some of you to clarify a point. Since I've been asked to present to you, I'll do my best to give the rest of you a working knowledge of X.")

It's up to you to claim your authority. Once you're in front of the audience, there's no way for you to earn it. Don't waste your time trying to earn it; doing that is a treadmill to oblivion. When I was an actor, we would refer to this as *still auditioning for the role.* In other words, the actor had auditioned for the role, had been given the part, had rehearsed it for weeks with the rest of the cast, and was now on stage performing it in front of an audience, but behaving as though he were still auditioning for the role. In that situation, the audience is not allowed to believe in the performance of the actor, because the actor doesn't believe in it.

Another common reason for saying too much is the illusion on the part of the presenter that the audience is *so interested* in what she's saying that she has to tell them every single thing she knows about the subject. This is especially common when a presenter's expertise is in a subject not well known by the general public. The public's unfamiliarity with your subject may be because they're intimidated by it. Don't intimidate them further by overwhelming them with too much information. The presenter can be so excited that people actually seem to be interested in her subject that she can go on endlessly. It's important to start developing a feedback mechanism that lets you *take the audience's temperature* in terms of how much is enough, and how much is too much. A rule that can help distill your message and material is: *Show them the nuggets, don't show them the ore.* The audience probably don't care about how much ore you had to remove from the stream; they just want to see the nuggets. By distilling your information, and letting them know that you're respectful of their time and attention, you increase the chance that you'll have their interest and that they will stay with you for your entire presentation. Remember the statement, "Show me your best slide?" That came from a man who was tired of being shown ore, who didn't have time to look at ore, and who was only interested in nuggets. Don't make your audience wish they were getting nuggets; just give the nuggets to them.

Ideally, when you finish, you want the audience to wish that you'd keep talking. The last thing in the world you want is for them is to think, "Isn't this ever going to end?" In that situation, the audience, or at least part of it, haven't heard a big percentage of what you've said. It's always better to be too brief than to go on for too long. If they want to know more, and there's still time, they can ask for it. If you've been asked to talk for half an hour, no one is going to complain if you finish early. If you've been asked to talk for half an hour, don't, under any circumstances, decide that you can talk for thirty-five minutes, or forty minutes, or for as long as you want. A half an hour *means a half an hour.* Besides, even if you've given the audience permission to ask questions, it's likely that there'll be questions at the end. The half hour time slot you've been given to present includes question and answer time at the end. If you've rehearsed properly (and I'll be talking about that soon) you'll have some idea of how long your presentation is. Always have a watch or clock in sight so that you can track the amount of time you have left.

The worst thing you can do is to have no idea of how long your presentation is, and to pay no attention to the amount of time that you've been given. This makes you look like you have no respect for the audience member's time. Think of it this way: If you've been given a half hour, and instead you talk for forty-five minutes, or an hour, and you have fifty people in the audience, you've just taken twelve-and-a-half hours, or twenty-five hours, of other people's time that doesn't belong to you. You're being a time bandit, and it's a good way to generate resentment in your audience.

If you've used your allotted time, including the time you had set aside for questions, and the audience is still bristling with unanswered questions that they seem to be dying to have addressed, you can say, "We've used up the time we've been given, but I'm willing to take more questions if you're able to stay." You can only do this if the audience is actually clamoring for more from you, and if you make sure that the room isn't promised to someone else (and if you have the time). If you're not able to answer all the questions, it's great if you're able to give the questioners your contact information, or some way to reach you so their questions can be answered. That way, they don't feel shortchanged.

If you're speaking at the end of a long day, or long evening, it's even more important that you *show them the nuggets* and be brief. In those circumstances, I often start my presentation with the words I know will sound sweetest to the audience: "I'll be brief." Openly acknowledging the fatigue of the audience will go a long way toward securing their good will. It shows that you're concerned for their well-being, and that you want to make it as easy and comfortable for them as you can. In other words, it lets them know that you inhabit the same universe they do, not some parallel universe.

If you know your story, you can tell it briefly. Remember the story of the man who had been promised forty-five minutes to tell his story, and ended up with five minutes? He succeeded not only because he was clear on his three goals, but also because he knew his story, and was able to expand or contract it to adapt to changing circumstances. Show them the nuggets, don't show them the ore.

CHAPTER 17:

Giving the Same Presentation Over and Over

Sometimes, you'll be in a position where you have to give the same basic presentation over and over, each time to a new audience. This can be difficult for presenters, especially when they focus on how tired they've become of repeatedly giving what feels like the same presentation. For the audience, though, the presentation is brand new each time. They've probably never seen it. If you subconsciously signal them that you're tired of it, you're essentially modeling the behavior that you expect from them. On a subconscious level, you're suggesting to them that they should be exhausted by it, too, and they will be. This is one of the things that actors learn when they're doing the run of a play, and have to act the same role every night. It's always a new audience though, and actors learn how to make it new every night, so it's not just new for the audience, it feels new for the actors, too. This is the same for touring musicians who have to sing the same hit song every night on tour. Eventually, they learn how to make it new for themselves each time they sing it.

A presenter can do the same thing. The first key I've already mentioned; the audience members have never seen your presentation. It's brand spanking new to them. Remember that. They always deserve the best you have. The second key is to adjust your goals to the specific circumstances you find yourself in. Even if you have to give the presentation six times in one day, the goals can be changed subtly. In fact, if you're really tuned in to your audience and the specific circumstances of each separate presentation, the goals will have to change, sometimes dramatically.

The first goal (*What do I want to walk away with?*) is the one you have the most flexibility with. If I had to give the same presentation six times in one day, my first goal would be "I want to walk away feeling like I was able to share even more passion about this subject than the first time I gave the presentation." Or, "I want to walk away feeling like I can make any presentation new for myself no matter how many times I have to give it." If you feed yourself this type of goal, you can transform the situation from drudgery to pleasure. You can also adjust the second goal (*What do I want the audience to walk away with?*) As a matter of fact, if you're being totally honest with yourself, you probably will have to adjust the second goal *every single time you give what seems like the same presentation,* even if the change is only by a small degree. Here's the long and short of it: it's always brand new for the audience, and you'd probably rather have it be new for you, too, right? Why bore yourself? Use the two keys that I've mentioned to find a way to make it new each time you give it. Being able to do this will make you a much better overall presenter, and when you're in a position to give a different presentation, it'll seem easy.

CHAPTER 18:

Pacing and Breathing

It's very seldom that I see a presenter who's going too slowly. Almost invariably, if there's an issue with pacing, it's because the person presenting is going too fast. That's what nervousness does; it gets presenters all jacked up, and they lose an accurate sense of what comfortable pacing feels like. Here's what happens when you go too fast: the audience get left behind. Very simply, they're not able to process the words that are coming at them too fast, so they're slightly behind you. It feels to them like they're *chasing after your bus* but never able to get on board. They won't chase you for long. They'll become frustrated, and quit the chase. In other words, they'll go back into their own, personal realities. Talking too fast is another way to ensure that you won't get enough oxygen, which at the least means you'll have trouble thinking straight. At worst, you'll become hypoxic, which is a sure road to panic. When I say, "Take your time," it has a very different meaning than saying, "Go slowly." *Taking your time* means honoring the pace at which humans can receive information, and honoring the pace at which humans (specifically you, the presenter) can comfortably deliver information. Here's a strange fact: A twenty-minute presentation delivered at a leisurely pace will seem shorter than a ten-minute presentation delivered at too fast a pace. The whole point of giving a presentation is making sure the audience gets your point. If you speak too fast, they won't get it, so it becomes entirely self-defeating to race through your presentation.

If you find you have less time than you thought, focus on the most important things you need to say, and let the rest fall away. Trying to make up for lack of time by talking fast will absolutely defeat you. You may get to say everything you'd planned, but the audience won't walk away with much.

Too much caffeine (or other drugs) can sometimes be the culprit. If you're cranked up on too much caffeine, you'll have a false sense of how fast you're speaking, or of how fast you should be speaking. Presenters sometimes use caffeine to *get themselves up* before they have to go on, and it can work too well. The result might feel great to you, but to the audience, it looks like you're completely out of control, and you are. Remember, the audience don't want to have the sense that you're out of control; it sabotages the authority you actually have. On top of that, it gives them no reason to stay with you, and every reason to abandon the reality that you're working so hard to set up.

As long as I've mentioned caffeine, I might as well talk about other drugs. None of them will enhance the experience of the audience. They may give you the illusion of enhancing *your* experience, but remember, it's not about your experience, it's about the experience of the audience. You have a responsibility, both to the audience and to yourself, to be at your best. I've actually heard people say how they're much better in front of an audience after they've had a couple of drinks. That won't be the audience's experience. The same thing with taking any drug *to calm you down*. It's throwing one too many variables into the mix. Besides, there'll be a time when you find yourself without your *mother's little helper,* and you'll still have to give your presentation. You won't really be able to say, "Well, I can't present right now, because I don't have my medication with me" will you?

If you need to calm yourself down before a presentation, try some deep breathing. The sort of breathing that I'm referring to involves an exhalation that's at least twice as long as your inhalation (even longer than that is better). The long exhalation is the key. Otherwise, you can easily hyperventilate. This sort of breathing is the basis for martial arts, yoga, and many sorts of meditation breathing. It's worked for centuries, and will absolutely work for you. There's a physiological basis for this sort of breathing. When you're anxious, your sympathetic nervous system takes over. This is the one that's been called the *fight or flight* system, and it gets you into a panic. Deep breathing with long exhalations allows your body *to switch over* to the parasympathetic nervous system, which has been called the *rest and digest* system. You'll feel yourself relax in a dramatic way after only a few minutes.

Practice long-exhalation breathing before you need it, so it becomes comfortable to you. I've found the best way to do it is to gently hum on the exhalation at about the same pitch as your normal speaking voice. The purpose of the hum is to give you a physical reminder that you're setting up a breathing pattern different than your usual one. Without the humming, the next thought that comes into your head will make you forget about deep breathing. One or two deep breaths aren't enough; you have to breathe this way for at least a few minutes before it has any effect. Try this the next time you find yourself feeling upset or scattered. Driving in your car is a great place to practice it. Once you're used to it, you'll be able to do it without humming so you won't call unnecessary attention to yourself if you're waiting to give a presentation in a room full of people. The beauty of this tool is that you always have it with you. (If you don't have it with you, it means you're not breathing and not alive. In that case, you won't need it.)

After you've gotten used to this, if you're in a situation where you can't hum, you can substitute a slight rasp in your breath. The people around you won't be able to hear it, but you'll be able to hear and feel it, so you'll be physically anchored to your breath, and you'll be able to stay calm and think clearly.

One last word about breathing: no one ever believes in how completely effective this technique is until they really try it. I'm used to seeing people's eyes glaze over when I start talking about breathing, and I can almost hear them thinking, "I already know how to breathe." I'm sure that's true, but you may not know how to use what you already know how to do in order to liberate you from almost any nervousness.

Back to speaking too fast, which erodes your authority as a presenter. When I see someone racing through a presentation, my first thought is, "Who are you trying to convince?" Speaking too fast doesn't serve anyone. It doesn't get more done in a shorter time, as some presenters think: it actually gets less done because it creates a situation where it's more difficult for the audience to comprehend and absorb what the presenter is saying. I've mentioned that it can also cut you off from your oxygen supply and make you panic, but it's worth repeating. The key to getting more done in a shorter time is to cut the body of your presentation down to the essentials. In other words, we're back to *show them the nuggets*. One of your jobs as a presenter is to make the audience feel comfortable. Talking too fast will put them on edge, and will make them less accessible and receptive to you. The final point about pacing is that you'll always have all the time you need, as long as you match the amount that you include in your presentation with the time you have. After a while, you'll learn how to do this automatically, even if you're asked *on the spot* to speak for three minutes. I can't say it often enough: Show them the nuggets; don't show them the ore.

CHAPTER 19:

The Power of Stillness and Silence

The same impulse that makes presenters tend to speak too fast can also make them feel that they have to keep up an unbroken stream of speech, with no pauses. In other words, the very powerful element of silence is completely missing from their presentation. It's all just words, words, words. I'm talking of silences that might last only a matter of a second or two, but provide natural breaks from one thought or subject to another. Their real power is that they give the audience time to process the information and content coming from the presenter. Pauses also give you time to think. A great deal of thinking can be done in two seconds. Remember, a lot of the mental processing done by the audience is on a subconscious level and happens very quickly. Sometimes, a second or two is all they need for what you've just said to *get into* their minds. (Just to put that into perspective, the conscious mind has been estimated to process input at a rate of two thousand bits per second. The unconscious mind works much faster. As a matter of fact, it's been estimated to work at a rate of four billion bits per second, or two million times faster than the conscious mind. This is one of the reasons I'm always saying that audiences are very smart on a subconscious level. Just like you, they know a great deal more than they realize. The difference between *knowing* and *thinking* is vast.) Being aware of this processing speed may allow you to see the value of small pauses. A great deal can be comprehended by the audience during a pause of a second or two. An additional benefit for you is having time to swallow so your throat doesn't get too dry, which gives you the look of being out of control. A constant stream of speech won't give you this chance; an occasional pause will.

Pauses accomplish several other important tasks. They give you time to breathe, they give you time to check the eyes of your audience for comprehension so you're sure that they're still *with you*, and they make you look confident and comfortable in your own skin. If you don't appear to have this kind of comfort, you're giving the audience an excuse not to believe anything you say. And finally, pauses allow audience members to fill in the blanks for themselves, in other words, to personalize the information being presented to them.

Acting and giving presentations are very different in a number of ways, but very similar in others. Think of specific actors who have the ability to really cast a spell over their audience. Actors who can do this tend to use silence and stillness very effectively. It makes them appear to have mastery over time and space. I'm not referring to the style of acting or comedy where the performer simply wears the audience down with manic energy. This could be called the *stun gun school of acting*. It sacrifices power in favor of overwhelming the audience. The equivalent to the style of acting I just mentioned is the infomercial style, the, "But wait, don't answer that – *now* what would you pay?" style you see on cable television. Unfortunately, silence and stillness are becoming less common in our culture. That doesn't make them any less powerful, in fact it makes them all the more powerful. Constant movement, pacing back and forth, and talking (usually too fast) without pause will always decrease what the audience is able to receive and process. In addition, this style doesn't leave any blank spaces for the audience members to fill in, so they aren't able to personalize the presentation and make it their own.

CHAPTER 20:

Casual Style vs. Casual Intent

This leads me directly into our next topic, casual style versus casual intent. Presenters commonly confuse these two things, and always to their disadvantage. We live in a society that's becoming more casual all the time. That's just fine, and there's no doubt this makes life easier in a lot of ways. When presenters confuse casual style and casual intent, it can give the audience the idea that the presenter isn't committed to the ideas or information, or point of view he is presenting. The result is there seems to be nothing at stake, and no reason to believe what the presenter is saying, or no reason to take it seriously. Being serious about your intention is vital if you expect to be listened to or taken seriously. In your presentation, your style can be as casual as you like, but your intention has to be ironclad.

Think of this as the iron hand in the velvet glove. The iron hand is your intention; the velvet glove is your style. For those of you who still may be a little confused about the word "intention," what I mean is being clear on your goals (and you will be, because you will have answered the three questions before you begin preparing your presentation). Whatever the answers to the questions may be, they have to add up to some version of "I have something I believe in and that the audience needs, something of vital importance to them, and I'm committed to getting it across to them." The opposite of this, which comes through when people confuse casual style with casual intent is some version of, "You can listen to this if you want, but you don't have to, because what I have to offer isn't really important to me or to you." If you feel this way about a presentation, don't give it until you've gotten your *mind right* about it. As I said earlier, a presentation is an expression of respect for the audience on many levels. If your intention is too casual, you signal them that you don't respect them, don't respect their time, don't believe in what you're saying, and don't expect them to believe in it either. This is a waste of your time, and theirs. Your time is too precious to waste, just like theirs is. Be clear about your intention, and be ironclad in that clarity. Then you can adopt a casual style, and it will work well for you.

Part of the impulse behind wanting to appear to be casual is tied up in the desire that many of us have to be thought of as being *cool,* which is another way of saying we want the acceptance of others. This desire for acceptance can make people act in a way that cuts them off from their passion. If you don't feel passionate about your subject, how can you possibly expect the audience to feel passionate about what you're saying? If they don't feel some level of passion, there's no way you're going to change them at all, and remember, you're there to change them on some level. Adopting a style that's only *cool* keeps the stakes low, and the audience gets the impression you have nothing to lose, and they have nothing to gain. Remember when I talked about how you had to first give the audience what you want in order to get the same back from them, that you have to model that behavior to them? Your willingness to show your passion is the only chance you have of infecting the audience with that same level of passion. Just to be clear, when I talk about letting your passion come through, I'm not talking about behaving like a revival tent preacher. Passionate presenters can be subtle in their style and still achieve dramatic results.

CHAPTER 21:

How it Looks vs. How it Feels

How it looks versus how it feels is so closely related to the casual intent/ casual style issue that this is a good time to talk about it. Because most of us can be nervous when we're up in front of an audience, we tend to focus on the experience we're having. Our nervousness makes us feel we're having a bad experience, and we project that onto the audience and wrongly think they're having the same experience. In other words, we confuse how it feels to us with how it looks to them. The two things couldn't possibly be any more different. I've already talked some about how presenters adopt one of two essential frames of focus. The first is *the outward focus* where you're completely connected to your audience and concentrating on their needs, and on your need to accomplish the goals you've set for yourself. This is the focus that allows you to be most like yourself (because you're not crippling yourself with self-consciousness). The second is *the inward focus,* where your entire concentration is taken up by your doubts about yourself, your nervousness and worrying that you're not good enough, and so on. This is the focus that keeps you from being your full, brilliant self. It keeps you as a *universe of one* because – by your focus, and subsequent lack of connection to the audience, you aren't able to really *be yourself* or to *let them in.*

It's liberating to realize the audience members aren't having the same experience you are. As a matter of fact, that realization can set you free. Coming to grips with this truth is absolutely essential for your development as a presenter. In the end, what you, the presenter, may be feeling simply doesn't matter. This isn't to minimize your nervousness, or your emotional state; they feel extremely real when you're about to present or are presenting to an audience. They just don't matter in terms of what you can actually accomplish. There are people who say that unless you're nervous, you can't give a good presentation. I'm not one of them. I don't believe that for a minute, and I don't want you to believe it either. Understand that the people in the audience aren't feeling what you're feeling. What you're feeling ultimately doesn't matter. Once you accept this, you're on the road to shedding your nervousness like a coat that doesn't fit anymore.

Sometimes the audience can see your nervousness; sometimes they can't. It doesn't matter either way. If they can see that you're nervous, but they see you're committed to connecting with them, to revealing yourself to them, to sharing your passion with them and making sure you achieve your goals, your nervousness won't matter to them. As a matter of fact, they may even identify with you more strongly, because they'll all be able to remember a time when they were nervous in front of an audience. Seeing your determination to get your message across to them, they'll admire you even more.

A productive way for you to think about any fear or nervousness you have is to think, "They'll see what I choose for them to see." This allows you to concentrate on what you need to accomplish, and on your connection with the audience. Putting your focus on any negative emotional state you may be feeling only gives that state the power to grow, and to take on a life of its own. In other words, concentrating on your emotional state feeds that state, gives it strength, and ultimately perpetuates the negative emotion. Focus on what you want: Connection with the audience, and attainment of your goals. In the larger picture, *how it feels to you is unimportant.* Don't give it power it doesn't really have.

CHAPTER 22:

Crafting Your Concluding Statement

When we were talking about opening statements, I said that the only part of a presentation people pay less attention to than the opening was the closing statement. The result is, most presentations don't really finish, they just stop, and usually, badly. Regardless of how powerful the presentation may have been up until that point, by not knowing how to end, and by just petering out, presenters rob themselves of both authority, and the momentum they've worked hard to build. The conclusion of a presentation is the section presenters most often expect to somehow magically take care of itself. It won't, so don't expect it to.

By the time you get to the end of your presentation, you've done a tremendous amount of work, both in terms of preparation and delivery. There's no need to throw it away by failing to wrap it all up in a nice package with a bow on it. This is an opportunity to let your audience know you've honored your commitment to them, and given them what you promised. In other words, it's one more opportunity for you to show respect for your audience. It's also your last chance to recap the important points you've made, the ones which encapsulate your message, and which you'd like the audience to remember. You can't afford to let an audience walk away from your presentation thinking, "She made four terrific points, but I can only remember two of them, and I'm not sure I have one of those right."

When we talked about opening statements, you may remember I suggested you write it out and memorize it. The same is true for the closing statement. We talked about standing in front of an audience, and thinking you knew what you were going to say only to find your mind was completely blank. The same thing is likely to happen at the end if you haven't prepared properly. It can be difficult to know how to stop talking, so typically, speakers just keep going on and on and on. It reminds me of a horror movie with multiple false endings. You think the movie is over, then the dead body sits back up with a knife in its hand. Somehow that gets resolved, and then Dracula breaks through the wall, and the situation keeps getting worse, and it seems like the movie will never end.

Painful as that experience is, watching a speaker who doesn't know how to end his talk is even worse. One of the endings I hear most often is, "That's all I've got." This is often accompanied by an apologetic shrug. If you're going to end this way, you may as well come right out and say, "Don't take anything I just said seriously." Remember, as the speaker, you're there to take care of the audience. They shouldn't have to worry about you, and they'll be worried if they sense you don't know how and when to end your talk. Make it easy for yourself and for them. Write out your closing statement, and memorize it. It only has to be a couple of lines. It can be something as simple as, "There are three things I'd like you to remember about having heard me. They are…" Or it can be a call to action, for example, "When you leave here today, I'd like you to…" Whatever your closing is, make it concise and definite. It's also useful to end with the words, "Thank you," by which you signal the audience that you're done. Once you're thanked them, leave them enough time to for them to applaud before you say, "I'll be happy to answer any questions you have." Otherwise, you can step on your own applause, which, after all, you've earned. By ending this decisively, you complete the impression that you know what you're talking about, and you're comfortable with your authority, so they can be too.

CHAPTER 23:

Rehearsing

In my experience, very few people understand either the value of rehearsing, or how to make the most of it. The result is that rehearsal
is not used at all, or is misused in a way that can do more harm than
good. In the first case, (and this is especially true of team rehearsals,
where a group of people present together) people talk about what
they're going to do instead of actually doing it. The impulse to substitute talking about what you're going to do instead of just doing it has
multiple origins. Embarrassment is one of them. People are simply em-
barrassed to present in front of their colleagues. It's easy to understand
this. Your colleagues tend to be some of your most merciless critics.
So, rather than actually rehearsing, people say things like, "And then
Bill will talk about the future vision of the company, and then Sharita
will gives some financial projections, and then I'll make the closing
remarks." This isn't rehearsing. In fact, it has absolutely nothing to
do with rehearsing. A justification I often hear for doing this is, "We
don't have the specific information yet." I've even seen people put off
getting the specific information they need for a team presentation for
as long as they can so they can avoid rehearsing. When they give their
presentation, no one really knows what the others are going to do, so
crucial points fail to be made, transitions are sloppy, and the presentation can drag on forever without accomplishing anything. The result
is that the team doesn't look like a team, and often doesn't accomplish
what it hoped to. Remember, part of giving any group presentation is
instilling confidence in the audience that you're really a team, so you'd
better look like a team.

Another misuse of rehearsing involves *setting* it word for word,
and gesture for gesture. The misguided impulse behind this kind of
rehearsing is that everything will be all right as long as the presenter
can control what's happening. Remember what I said a while back:

However you think your presentation will go, it won't. Get used to this. Trying to make your presentation about perfection just drains the life out of it.

When a presentation is overly-controlled, the presenter has the illusion of control, but the audience feel like they're watching a very sophisticated robot. There's no life in the presenter or the presentation; it's all been drained out by *rehearsal*, so the audience have no reason to migrate to your reality. They stay in their own mental worlds. By the way, this last sort of rehearsing often involves the use of a mirror for the presenter to rehearse in front of. I'm going to be as emphatic as I can about this: never, ever rehearse in front of a mirror. I understand people want to know what they look like when they're giving a presentation. I also understand people would like to have the same experience when they're giving a presentation as they have when they watch someone else giving a presentation. Accept the truth: the two things are completely different. You'll never have the same experience watching as doing. Accepting this will help set you free as a presenter.

When you watch yourself in a mirror, you're presenting the face you want and expect to see. We all do this, by the way. It's the reason why if you happen to catch sight of yourself in a store window or some other reflective surface, you can be surprised to the point of thinking, "Is that me? I didn't think I looked like *that*." You were surprised by the way you looked because you hadn't consciously composed the picture, the way we invariably do when we know we're about to see our own reflections in the mirror. The fact is, when you watch yourself rehearse in a mirror, you're unconsciously editing and censoring, making tiny adjustments in order to see the version of yourself that comes closest to the way you'd like to see yourself. That sort of censoring and editing takes away the spontaneity an audience most want to see, and it drains all the life out of you. In a strange way, you're doing an imitation of yourself for the mirror. It's not an imitation that other people will recognize as the interesting, full human being you are. Looking at a mirror, you're not watching your real self rehearse, you're watching your ego rehearse. I feel the same way about watching videotaped recordings of rehearsals or presentations. They seem like a good idea, but they're generally counter-productive. Invariably, when we watch videotapes of ourselves, we focus on those physical qualities we like least about ourselves, and that's all we see. "I'm so fat, I'm so skinny, I'm so bald, I'm so hairy, my nose looks so big, my nose looks so small," and so on. People who are accustomed to seeing themselves on videotape tend to avoid watching their own presentations or performances. This is especially true of actors, who almost never like to watch themselves. They know better. On some level they understand that the dissonance between the way it feels to them, and the way it looks to an audience can never be resolved. They also understand that focusing on how they look is absolutely the wrong place to focus. It fosters self-consciousness, which always cuts you off from the audience.

Most people have no idea of how they're seen by others. I said earlier I often tell clients that after I've talked to them for just a few minutes that I have a better idea of how they appear to others than they'll ever have, because I have an objective view, and I know what I'm looking at. You don't need to know how you appear to others. It's essentially unknowable, and it's not information that will get you anything at all, other than to make you feel self-conscious, which will disconnect you from your audience.

Another misuse, or actually, non-use of rehearsal is the, "I'll just wing it" school of preparation. I've seen this happen when someone is dreading the thought of having to give a presentation to the point where they don't even want to think about preparing. It can also happen when a person has a sense of being a better presenter than he or she really is. (This is common, by the way. Getting accurate feedback about how well you gave a presentation is extremely hard. Most people, when asked for feedback will just say, "I thought it was fine." There are several possible reasons for this. The first is that they may not be good objective judges. Few people are. The second is that they often feel they can't tell you what they really think.) Presenters can also have an inaccurate view of how good they are when they confuse just getting through a presentation with giving a good presentation. So what passes for preparation or rehearsal becomes a fantasy in which the presenter imagines himself giving a presentation, complete with snappy phrases. In that frame of mind, fresh from a successful presentation fantasy, it can be easy to think you're ready to stand up and present. This fantasy always involves what you're going to say, it almost never gets down to what you're trying to accomplish, in other words, it never gets down to actual goals, so it leaves you utterly unprepared to present.

The last common misuse of rehearsal I'll talk about is likely to happen when you actually run through the material for your presentation, and the run-though goes really well, and feels just great. One of the reasons it may have felt great to you is that you have given yourself over to achieving your goals, and you were so connected to them, you lost all sense of self-consciousness. It might have felt so easy and commanding that you had the illusion someone else was speaking through your mouth, which generally indicates an absence of self-consciousness. What can come from this sort of rehearsal is the desire to have exactly the same experience in the next run-through, or when you actually deliver the presentation. So you try to replicate exactly what you did last time, and it doesn't work. It feels like an imitation of life to you, and if you're in front of an audience when you attempt this sort of replication, they feel like it's an imitation of life, too, because that's exactly what it is.

Though being able to visualize yourself giving a great presentation can be useful, in a weird way, indulging in the fantasy of giving a great presentation can also be a version of living in the future, instead of the present. One of the common qualities of all great presenters is that when they're giving a presentation, they're absolutely and completely in the moment. They aren't living in the past or the future; they're in the moment, and so they're able to bring the audience into that moment. By doing this, they're able to create the *consensual reality* I spoke about earlier. You can never show the audience the real you in the past or the future, you can only through your willingness to be in the moment with the audience.

Now that we've gotten some of the misuses of rehearsal out of the way, let's talk about how to use rehearsal to full advantage. I talked a minute ago about what happens when you give yourself over to your goals and lose all sense of self-consciousness, about the feeling of having someone else talk with your mouth. (By the way, that *someone else* is the real you breaking through.) This sense of clarity and connection to your material, to your goals, and to your audience, is what you always want to strive for. Rehearsal only becomes a misuse when you try to recreate a feeling by repeating exactly what you did last time. When you try to recreate that feeling, you're trying to recreate a moment that's past. Rather than recreating the feeling, focus on recreating the experience of alignment and connection with your material, your goals, and your audience. Surrender any attachment to the idea that you can recreate the same feeling and the same moment. Each time you go through your presentation, it'll be different. That's what makes it a living thing; that's what makes it interesting and engaging to the audience. They'll know when you're serving up *repeated life* instead of real, spontaneous life, and they'll respond to it like they would if you were serving them five-day-old fish.

A phrase that might be helpful to set up the most productive mindset when you are starting to rehearse is, "Let's just see what it's like this time around." Get yourself ready for the idea that each time you run through your presentation, it'll be different from the last time you did it, and different from the next time you do it. The differences may be small, they may be large. As long as you're connected to your goals, material, and your imaginary audience, and are honoring the essential flow you've devised, you're doing just fine, and your focus is in the right place. Learn to think of the differences that appear each time you run your presentation as positive. That's where the life is, and that's one of the things that connects you to your audience. You're showing them real life, and they'll be grateful to you for it.

So that phrase, "Let's just see what it's like this time around" will go a long way toward setting up the right sort of expectations in your mind. I can't emphasize enough how important this sort of mindset is. It gets you ready to adapt to whatever might happen.

Now that we've gotten the "Let's see what it's like this time" mindset taken care of, it's time to talk about the mechanics of rehearsing. This is assuming you've started the right way, by answering the three questions that allow you to set your goals. You've also done whatever research was required, so you know your subject well enough to talk about it spontaneously. In addition, you've written your statement of intent, and because you know your goals, you're also able to write your closing statement. Now you've got a strong opening, and a strong finish, and all you need is that great big piece in the middle, which is actually the easiest part. We talked about crafting your flow earlier, so you also know the major points that you want to cover, and you know both the order in which you want to cover them, and the amount of detail you want to include. You've either made PowerPoint slides (just a warning again that unless you're conscious of the potential danger of slides, PowerPoint can be an obstacle standing between you and your audience) or you've made simple note cards with only one or two words about each point or sub-point you need to make. Now, just go for it, be willing to give it a try, and run through it.

As you do this, the most productive mental focus for you to adopt will be on your goals, and the flow of material. Sometimes, you'll find that you have to rehearse by yourself. This can actually be preferable to running through your presentation for someone who doesn't understand what they're seeing, or who knows you so well they are not in a position to be an objective audience. Most presenters feel vulnerable at this stage, which is perfectly all right. The potential problem comes when, in this state of vulnerability, you ask someone to judge your presentation. They may be in a position to help you, or they may not be. Ask for input at this point only if you feel you stand a good chance of getting helpful, constructive, actionable feedback, and only if you're able to take in that information from an objective, detached, non-personal perspective.

Don't ever talk yourself out of rehearsing just because you don't have an audience. You can still get a great deal of value out of rehearsing by yourself, if you do it properly. If you're rehearsing alone, with no one watching, it can be tempting to look in the mirror. I talked at length earlier about the danger of mirror rehearsal, but it's worth repeating. Don't do it. If you try to rehearse in front of the mirror, your focus will go inward, and you'll be judging yourself instead of trying to make an outward connection with an audience (even if the audience is imaginary.) It's much better to look at a wall, and build an imaginary audience in your mind. This can be a form of exercise that builds the *muscles* which allow you to connect to a real audience. When I take someone through a rehearsal of a presentation intended for a mass audience, I emphasize that we're in a slightly unnatural situation because their entire focus is on making a connection with me, and seeing comprehension in my eyes. By focusing on me, and using the same energy they would normally use to connect to multiple sets of eyes in an audience, I tell them that when they actually get in front of an audience, and have the luxury of looking into all those different eyes, it'll be much easier for them. The same is true of rehearsing to a wall. If you imagine you have an audience, and actually visualize them to the point where you're attempting to get your message across to them, you'll be amazed and relieved at how much easier it is for you when you have real faces with real eyes to look into.

Chapter 24:

Putting it All Together

Let's say you've just taken all the steps we've talked about. You can state your goals clearly and simply, you have a statement of intent, you've crafted a concluding statement, you've internalized the flow of your presentation and know exactly which points you need to cover, and how one point leads into the next. You've internalized this so well that if you're using slides or PowerPoint, you're ready to give the impression that the presentation is coming from you instead of from the slides. You're clear on your obligations to your audience, and you're ready to infect them with your passion. You've rehearsed, you understand your presentation will be slightly different from your rehearsal, and that's fine with you.

Now what? Now you're ready, that's all. You may not feel ready, but don't confuse being completely prepared with knowing how it will feel or how it will go. These elements are unknowable and have nothing to do with your level of preparedness. Even if there were a way to anticipate whatever surprises might occur, you'd be reducing your ability to respond in a spontaneous fashion. Remember, the surprises and your ability to react to them is where the real life is in your presentation. Embrace the sense of not knowing, and understand how it will enrich what you bring to your presentation. It will enrich both your experience, and the experience of your audience. Good luck, and feel free to contact me if I can be of help. My address is gary@spokenwordsolutions.com.

About the Author

For more than 19 years, Gary Stine has been a teacher, coach, and advisor to hundreds of highly accomplished professionals. Working with clients on a confidential, one-to-one basis, Gary has helped them to be able to reveal their true selves in the sort of public settings that generate fear in most of us. Directly addressing these fears, and going beyond them, as well as helping clients to develop concise, compelling, personal styles that display their unique strengths and connect them to their audiences are by-products of the coaching he provides.

In addition to working with individual clients, Gary's corporate clients have included top-tier executives and their teams from Johnson and Johnson, Goldman Sachs, Bristol-Myers Squibb, Rockwell International, Hill & Knowlton, Dunkin' Donuts, Jannsen Pharmaceutica, the RW Johnson Pharmaceutical Research Institute, Schering-Plough, Abbott Labs, C. R. Bard, Korn Ferry International, Reed Elsevier, and the United Nations Development Programme. He is the founder and principal of Spoken Word Solutions.

CPSIA information can be obtained at www.ICGtesting.com
Printed in the USA
BVOW04s0729031214

377474BV00005B/13/P